DATE DUE

PLANNING AND CONTROL FOR PROFIT

Ralph F. Lewis *General Partner,*
Arthur Young & Company

PLANNING AND CONTROL
FOR PROFIT

MANAGEMENT USES OF ACCOUNTING, REVISED EDITION

HARPER & ROW, PUBLISHERS

NEW YORK, EVANSTON, AND LONDON

1817

70 71 72 73 10 9 8 7 6 5 4 3 2

Dedicated to the four men who contributed the most
to my development in the formative years of my business life

Arnold W. Carlson
Harry W. Knight
Philip Donham
John L. Burns

and of course to Teddy, whose patience and understanding
during the months of this book's gestation have been
"above and beyond the call."

Contents

Preface, ix

Part I. Planning and Control

1. The Big Picture, 3
2. Planning, 6
3. Control, 13
4. Management Information Systems, 19

Part II. Management Uses of Accounting

5. The Uses and Limitations of Conventional Accounting Statements, 27
6. Marketing, 46
7. Producing the Goods, 66
8. Research and Development, 90
9. Administrative Costs, 98
10. Capital Budgeting, 106
11. Cash Management, 120

Part III. Management Uses of Operations Research

12. Operations Research as a Planning Tool, 133
13. An Inventory Problem: A Determinate Solution, 144
14. Handling the Risk Factor, 152
15. System Simulation, 163
16. Queuing Theory, 171
17. Statistical Inference, 181
18. Mathematical Programming, 192
19. Critical Path Scheduling, 205
20. The Usefulness of Operations Research in Planning and Control, 216

Bibliography, 219

Index, 223

Preface

This book has been written for the businessman. First, it is for the generalist, who personally directs all phases of his operations and makes all policy decisions which may make or break the enterprise. Second, it is for the specialist, whether in production, finance, marketing, or research, who feels the need to see how his function fits into the total business. It can also be useful to the neophyte who is trying to achieve a systematic understanding of the factors that make a business successful or unsuccessful.

We are attempting in this book to meld an old technique—accounting—with a relatively new one—Operations Research—and to demonstrate how they can be joined in planning and controlling a profitable business enterprise.

Although the practice of accounting has had a place in business operations for many years, it is often confused with simple bookkeeping. The very definition of accounting—answering for, or explaining—indicates that its role is a passive, after-the-fact one. Traditionally, the accountant wore a green eye shade and spent his time bent over a high desk recording what happened in the past. Small wonder that in the eyes of many people accounting is still only a necessary evil.

Only recently has it been recognized that accounting is a powerful and important tool of business management. Today's enlightened executive has a much more accurate view of the management uses of accounting in shaping both short- and long-range policy. Past results are of interest, but the real value of accounting lies in controlling current operations and in planning for the future.

Most large businesses now recognize the usefulness of accounting in managing far-flung and somewhat disparate activities. This awareness is reflected in the increasing use of budgetary controls over operations. Many medium-sized and smaller businesses, however, are still run on a "seat-of-the-pants" philosophy, and little use is made of accounting except as a means of determining income and taxes for each year.

Operations Research was first used successfully in any significant way by the military in World War II. Since that time, as often happens when a new technique comes onto the scene, it has had a checkered career. Much too much has been expected of Operations Research in some quarters, and as a result it is in some disrepute. On the other hand, where it is intelligently used and where its limitations are clearly recognized, it can be of material help in arriving at better answers to business problems.

The main purpose of this book is to show the reader how valuable accounting and Operations Research can be, if properly used, in charting the future and controlling the present activities of any business, large or small.

The author owes special gratitude to Victor Waese, who did much of the research in putting together the examples of Operations Research at work; to Dr. Harold Davidson, Senior Director of the Bethesda, Maryland, office of Arthur Young & Company; and Dr. Phillip Carlson, Professor of Business Administration at Emory University, both of whom reviewed the text and made valuable suggestions for improvement; and to Miss Rita Anton, whose work as administrative assistant made this book possible.

—RALPH F. LEWIS

New York City
January 1970

PART I

Planning and Control

1 The Big Picture

The first objective of any business, despite all that has been written and said about social or other aims, must be to make a profit. Without profits, a business will necessarily fail, and all other goals, no matter how praiseworthy, will be unfulfilled. And without debating what adequate profit margins are, it must be conceded that most businessmen feel the need for improvement.

Until recently, the major use of accounting has been historical. It has recorded the information necessary to prepare profit and loss statements and balance sheets. It has been used, in effect, as a means of reporting to management, stockholders, the general public, and the government what has happened in a business in the past. Although the importance of this function is unlikely to diminish in the future, the role of accounting as a tool for the management of a business is being increasingly recognized.

Operations Research came into prominence during World War II as an important factor in the war effort. Since that time, and despite considerable problems, it has proved to be of genuine potential for the businessman, particularly in planning where he wants to go and how he is to get there.

The point of this book is, simply, that the use of accounting and of Operations Research for planning and control can produce a better profit margin. Although a number of techniques that are helpful in this regard will be discussed, the long-range plan and the budget are the focal points of all activities; and our emphasis will be on these two areas.

The *long-range plan,* whether it be for two, three, five, or ten years, is in reality a set of guidelines for a business. The businessman charts his course, and then makes those immediate decisions which seem most likely to advance him toward his goal. As he receives his feedback (information on what is happening), he may modify some of his decisions or he may change his long-range goals. A word of caution is in order here. We have yet to see any businessman who, when first confronted with the idea of a long-range plan, does not react, "But my business is different. There are so many outside factors over which I have no control that I cannot make a long-range plan." Those same businessmen, after exposure to long-range planning, come to recognize that the very existence of a long-range plan is of great help to them in day-to-day decisions. In our dynamic world, however, no long-range plan should remain fixed. It should be reviewed at least once a year, preferably more often, and should be modified to take into consideration more recent events.

The *budget* is the process of expressing in units and dollars the plans for a business for a specific period of time, usually a year. It is the means by which the conflicting goals of various departments may be reconciled so that the best interests of the enterprise as a whole may be achieved. In a one-man operation, it may be possible to get by without reducing over-all plans to quantitative terms. On the other hand, even smaller businesses are becoming complex to the point that some systematic process of getting figures down on paper is increasingly essential if all areas of a business are to be harnessed for achieving over-all company aims.

In short, the long-range plan and the budget go hand in hand. The long-range plan is the vehicle for quantifying where a business should be headed and the best route to follow in order to arrive at that destination. This is the process of *planning.*

The budget indicates specific steps to be taken in the near future which will lead to accomplishment of the long-range plan. By comparing actual results with the budget, we can *control* our course of action as well as modify intermediate goals in the light of changing conditions.

2 Planning

Most businessmen at management level have a dual job: day-to-day operations and planning ahead. Because of the immediately compelling nature of day-to-day decisions, it is typical that these operations use up the bulk of the busy executive's time. As a result, planning frequently gets short shrift.

Any thinking executive should realize, however, that day-to-day decisions made without reference to long-range plans are even more time-consuming and may, in addition, be incompatible with the best interests of the business in the long run. Figure 2–1 indicates what might be ideal percentages of available time to be spent in future planning at the various echelons of a company. Of course, no company, no matter how large, now actually devotes this amount of attention to planning. Typically, where planning is done, it is organized in a department out of the mainstream, which must fight for the busy executive's attention.

Successful planning must be both qualitative and quantitative. For example, if you determine that you want to be the biggest seller of your products in the county, state, region, or country, you must translate this goal into sales dollars. If you say that you are aiming

Chairman
President
Executive vice-president
Vice-president
Division head
Department head
Assistant department head
Foreman
Lead man
Worker

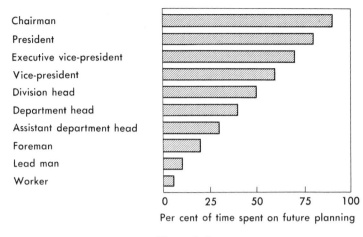

0   25   50   75   100
Per cent of time spent on future planning

Figure 2–1

for any given percentage of the total market for a like product, this, too, must be converted into actual sales for your product. When the production and marketing costs required to meet these sales goals are computed, this quantitative information might well bring about major changes in qualitative thinking.

Accounting is the handmaiden of planning. Without it, planning cannot be effective, since quantitative goals must be established throughout the company before decisions as to courses of action can be undertaken.

In preparing an over-all plan, the major objectives of a company should first be set forth. The company's policymakers must then answer in accounting (quantitative) terms such questions as the following:

1. What is a reasonable return on investment?
2. How can the company best go about getting this return?
3. What resources will be necessary to fulfill the plans decided upon?
4. How much of these resources can come from within the business?
5. How can additional resources be best obtained from outside the business?
6. How can all resources be best utilized to attain the company's objectives?

Determination of what a company's objectives should be is most often made by the chief executive officer, and frequently on subjective grounds. Although much can be done to improve the performance of business in setting objectives, this is a highly complex subject on which a great deal has already been written. Our subject is the translation of a company's objectives into workable plans and the use of proper controls to ensure that those plans are achieved.

A Typical Planning Problem

Let us consider a meat packing company that dresses and distributes beef, pork, and lamb throughout two states. The board of directors has voted to expand the line to include, if feasible, such specialty products as liverwurst, sausage, and bologna. Many of the subsequent planning steps may be taking place at the same time, but all departments of the business should be working on the project. Here are some of the assignments.

For the Production Department:

1. What products can be made at what costs—with varying levels of production?
2. What are the facilities problems—space and equipment?
3. What kinds and numbers of people would have to be hired to produce this new product?

For the Sales Department:

1. What are the wholesale and retail prices at which competing products are being sold?
2. Who are the major competitors, and how much do they sell to what customers?
3. Are there any peculiarities in the sales and distribution pattern of each of these products?

The interplay among the various elements of the business is obvious. For example, as the sales department finds potential markets, these must be translated into production requirements. As production finds bottlenecks, these must be worked out or sales plans must be changed.

These elements may well change in relative importance from time to time. For example, until early 1953 the limiting factor in television set sales was, by and large, productive capacity. Today, with the combination of increased capacity and partial market saturation, the major limitation is consumer demand.

Of all the elements to be considered, consumer demand is the least amenable to accurate forecasting. This means that, where possible, the plan adopted should allow maximum flexibility. Given a situation, for example, in which anticipated sales exceed productive capacity, it might be well to increase production by purchasing parts or assemblies from other companies, for a time at least, before expanding facilities.

In brief, before undertaking any steps to make and market the new products, the following cycle should be completed:

1. Decide on policy.
2. Prepare a plan.
3. Measure possible results.
4. Evaluate results.
5. Prepare a new plan.
6. Measure possible results.
7. Evaluate results.

Although steps 2, 3, and 4 (or 5, 6, and 7) may be repeated in whole or in part many times over, these steps constitute the formula for budgeting or profit planning. When a practical plan is produced that survives all tests in meeting the objectives, it is adopted.

A Representative Timetable

In most companies, budget preparation is an annual event. Here is a fairly typical budget timetable for a company on a calendar-year basis.

October 1. Management sets tentative broad goals in terms of return on investment or some other measure by product lines and furnishes over-all guidance as to general economic conditions expected in the coming year. Firm timetables are set for each department to submit its figures, with sales budgets due before others.

October 1–November 15. Salesmen and lowest-level supervisors prepare preliminary budgets for their operations and discuss them with their immediate supervisors. Supervisors modify and combine budgets and transmit them up through the organization. Accountants usually lend staff help by furnishing historical figures, coordinating the budget among the various departments, policing the timetable, consolidating results from the various areas, and generally overseeing the operation. As will be seen, it is essential that line supervisors have a major voice in preparing their own budgets.

November 15–December 1. Management reviews the preliminary budgets and, acting in the light of the results, suggests changes in objectives and assumptions. During this period each major department head has a session with top management, at which time his budget is discussed in detail.

December 1–December 15. Final budgets are prepared and consolidated. Top management takes the final budget to the board of directors for approval, and the approved budget is passed down through the organization.

We have defined a budget as a plan for a business which can in turn be used to control operations. In most situations, however, a static budget, even for as short a period as a year, becomes of decreasing value as the months pass because of changing conditions beyond the company's control. Many companies revise their budgets three times during the year (quarterly) and find they can retain good control.

The Flexible Budget

On the other hand, where customer demand is very uncertain, the case may be strong for a flexible budget, one that indicates alternative plans for variations in sales volume. In preparing a flexible budget, every expense must be analyzed to determine whether it is fixed (does not change with volume; for example, a foreman's salary), variable (will rise and fall with volume; for example, piece-work wages), or is semivariable (a mixture of fixed and variable). A flexible budget is in reality several different budgets, each reflecting a different level of productivity.

For example, a typical flexible budget in summary form for manufacturing costs for varying levels of productivity might look something like Table 2–1.

TABLE 2–1

Number of items produced	100,000	150,000	175,000	200,000
Manufacturing costs:				
Variable:				
Materials	$ 50,000	$ 75,000	$ 87,500	$100,000
Direct labor	25,000	37,500	43,750	50,000
Overhead	10,000	15,000	17,500	20,000
Semivariable:				
Supervision	10,000	10,000	16,000	16,000
Maintenance	5,000	10,000	10,000	10,000
Fixed:				
Depreciation	20,000	20,000	20,000	20,000
Total manufacturing costs	$120,000	$167,500	$194,750	$216,000
Cost per item produced	$1.20	$1.12	$1.11	$1.08

Budgeting in this way can be helpful by giving management a definite checkpoint to compare actual efficiency with that projected, and by pointing up the differences in costs resulting from volume changes. This latter information might well result in reconsideration of pricing policies.

Break-even Charts

One way of aiding management by providing facts on which decisions may be based is through the use of graphs. For example, flexible budgeting and the impact of varying levels of activity on the profitability of a business can be clearly shown on a break-even chart.

If Company X had an average net selling price of 66⅔ cents per item, yearly fixed expenses (management salaries, rent, depreciation, office overhead, etc.) of $150,000, variable expenses (materials and direct labor) of 20 cents per item, and semivariable expenses (indirect labor, plant maintenance, etc.) which increase steadily from $20,000 to $70,000 as production rises, the picture might be as shown in Figure 2–2.

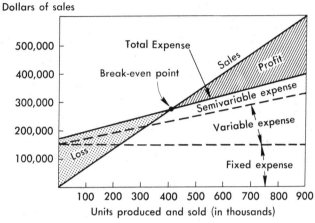

Figure 2–2. Break-even Chart—Company X

In this oversimplified example, the company will "break even" (have neither loss nor gain) on slightly less than $300,000 sales. If sales doubled to $600,000, profit would be in the neighborhood of $200,000. If sales were only $200,000, a loss of about $100,000 would result.

Summary

Too many businessmen today feel that they are subject to so many events outside their control that they must spend their entire time in reacting quickly to environmental changes. If they can move fast enough they are heroes; if they are sluggish, they are "bums."

The business which has a plan and whose executives base their short-term decisions on long-range effects is much more likely to succeed than one in which decisions are based on short-term effects.

3   Control

Control, like planning, is exerted in two ways, short-term and long-term. Handling short-term problems is simply "putting out fires." Here the basic aim is handling things on a day-to-day basis. A sales executive, for example, might be faced with the problem of how low to cut prices in order to land a sizable order, or a production man might have to decide whether or not to work overtime to get an order out. These are short-term decisions, but deciding each on its own may result in a confused pattern. On the other hand, if short-term decisions are made with a long-term plan in mind, they are more likely to result in concerted action toward a definite goal.

The ideal result, then, is the combination of planning for the long pull—subject to constant change as external conditions change—and control of day-to-day, month-to-month operations in accordance with the long-range plan.

In the previous chapter we discussed preparation of a company plan (budget). Budgets not only plan, however; they also serve to control operations.

All forecasts (one- to ten-year plans) and budgets (plans for up to one year) should be prepared to agree with the form in which financial results will be presented. This may mean major overhaul of financial statements. Here the size and degree of centralization of the business must dictate what sort of statements make most sense. In any case, budgets and actual results should be presented in a form consistent with the way in which responsibility for results is delegated.

Two basic techniques helpful in the use of accounting as a control tool are responsibility accounting and management by exception.

Responsibility Accounting

Charles L. Stillman, chairman of the finance committee of Time Inc., said some years ago: "A company moves from small company to big company status when it can afford a top-notch man to handle each of the major functions—sales, production, research, and finance."

If you are a "big company," the form of your statements will vary markedly from that of the company in which one man makes all the decisions. Regardless of size, however, forward planning can make sense only if the lowest level of supervision is brought into the act. Moreover, statements should be drawn up so that the man responsible for bringing in or spending money is accountable for his own operation. This practice, called "responsibility accounting," is fundamental but often neglected. Its premise is that responsibility and authority must go together for efficient operation. A couple of examples may be helpful in showing how responsibility accounting works.

EXAMPLE I: SALES EXPENSES. Company X has five sales regions, each in the charge of a regional manager. Each manager hires and fires his own salesmen and other employees and, in effect, runs his own office. Since all the regions sell the same product, the corporate accounting statements for selling expenses contain the following accounts:

Salaries
Expenses—selling
Office overhead

This consolidated report makes simple reading, but gives the regional managers no tools for control. The ideal statement, prepared separately for each region, might well specify:

Salesmen's salaries
Clerical salaries
Salesmen's expenses
Rent
Light
Telephones and telegraph
Miscellaneous

If the regional managers are called upon to prepare their own budgets for what they need, they are much more likely to live within the budgets, particularly if they receive regular reports from headquarters on how they are doing.

EXAMPLE II: FACTORY OVERHEAD. All too often, factory overhead is lumped into catchall accounts such as supervision, maintenance, supplies, setup time, timekeepers, etc., and foremen are charged only with getting out quantities of product. Under responsibility accounting, a foreman receives his own accounting statement periodically, listing amounts spent on items under his control against his budget. It is surprising how many short-cuts are found in such areas as setup time, maintenance, supplies used, etc., when the foreman knows he will be held specifically accountable for all operations for which he has authority.

Every item on a profit and loss statement should be the clear-cut responsibility of one person. Only by balancing responsibility and authority can maximum efficiency be obtained.

Management by Exception

The second cornerstone of control is the use of *management by exception*. No matter how busy management may be, the bulk of its time should be spent in planning for the future. Then as events develop, no time need be spent on those going according to plan. Attention can be devoted to those items which are varying from the plan.

Too often, presidents and boards of directors are furnished imposing books full of statements, in which no attempt is made to sort out what is going according to plan, what are the important deviations, and why. If planning is well done, events of a month may well be reflected in a one-page statement—and corrective action is more likely to take place.

A Typical Control Problem

It may be worthwhile, in examining planning and control, to look at some typical financial statements of a well-run diversified company.

In Table 3–1 you will note that the time-honored comparison of this month with the same month last year and year to date on the same basis has been eliminated. The plan (budget) has taken into consideration all past history, but has modified it by current considerations; hence, the historical information, having been thoroughly discounted, is of no value at this time.

TABLE 3–1

OVER-ALL INCOME STATEMENT
(In thousands)

Current Month			Year to Date	
Actual	Budget	Division	Actual	Budget
$1,089	$ 750	Components	$ 4,148	$ 3,500
1,549	1,850	Consumer products	6,380	7,250
2,850	2,700	Government products	11,262	11,600
2,162	2,100	Industrial products	10,091	9,600
$7,650	$7,400		$31,881	$31,950
1,105	1,200	Corporate expenses	4,398	4,500
$6,545	$6,200	Income before taxes	$27,483	$27,450
3,200	3,000	Income taxes	13,401	13,250
$3,345	$3,200	Net income	$14,082	$14,200

Obviously, the consumer products division is in trouble. Although we may want the head of the division to attend the board meeting, we shall certainly want to look at a divisional earnings statement. Here is the statement of the consumer products division.

TABLE 3–2
INCOME STATEMENT
CONSUMER PRODUCTS DIVISION
(In thousands)

| Current Month | | | Year to Date | |
Actual	Budget	Division	Actual	Budget
$7,164	$ 7,100	TV sales	$30,080	$29,950
2,721	3,750	Radio & phono sales	10,652	13,550
$9,885	$10,850	Total sales	$40,732	$43,500
6,919	7,600	Cost of goods sold	28,620	30,550
$2,966	$ 3,250	Gross profit	$12,112	$12,950
1,417	1,400	Selling, advertising & administrative expense	5,732	5,700
$1,549	$ 1,850	Divisional income before corporate expenses and income taxes	$ 6,380	$ 7,250

A review of a further underlying statement—in this case a comparison of actual and budgeted sales geographically and by product line—revealed that radio sales in the eastern region had not lived up to expectations. The action then taken reversed this trend within sixty days.

This swift action can only be taken if the trouble spot can be located quickly (management by exception), and a finger can be put on who is responsible (responsibility accounting).

Summary

A budget is merely the reduction of a company's plans to quantitative terms. However, in the course of translating over-all plans into units of production, numbers of employees, units of time, and dollar revenues and expenses, modifications of departmental plans are often found necessary, in order to produce the best over-all results. Moreover, a budget may reveal that the results to be expected from management's plans are inadequate and that plans should be revised. The use of accounting in charting the course of a business can be most important.

On the other hand, the best plans are of no value unless action is taken to translate them into reality. Every person who can influence profits should have authority in his own sphere but should be held strictly accountable for his operations. The budget, constructed so that every supervisor is held accountable for his own operation, is the key to making sure that plans become realities. And accounting is the means by which management can exert control.

4 Management Information Systems

Much attention has been paid in recent years to Management Information Systems (MIS). As a result, many managers are hip-deep in computer runs and have far more information than they can ever use, let alone assimilate. The whole subject needs some definition.

Certainly, it is clear that management cannot run its business well unless it understands its resources—present and potential, its customers, and its production and distribution processes. Information on these subjects is important for planning, controlling, and evaluating performance. Thus, it seems essential to develop a coordinated body of methods and procedures to measure important activities and to communicate the measurements to management.

Ideally, every decision maker should instantaneously receive all information about every activity influencing performance for which he is responsible. Upon receiving such information, he can, in theory, make strategic judgments, based upon current trends, and win a greater share of the market, cut his costs, or operate more efficiently in general.

Good as this arrangement sounds on paper, some practical restraints operate against this idyllic situation:

1. Managers can absorb only so much information; and when they are deluged with data, it becomes increasingly difficult for them to determine what is important. The poor manager can spend so much time poring over data that he becomes a prisoner of the system, and loses his discriminative judgment. Or, he may rebel against all the data presented and try to "fly by the seat of his pants."

2. Information costs money. It takes time to retrieve, organize, and communicate information. To furnish the manager complete data on all facets of his operation may be prohibitively costly.

3. Some activities are resistant to measurement. The effectiveness of advertising, the amount of money to be spent productively in research, and the success of training programs are a few examples of areas which are extremely difficult to evaluate on any kind of current basis.

4. Some kinds of information are just not available on a current basis. What competitiors are doing, what is happening or is likely to happen to the general economy, and the changing frame of mind of the consumer are some of these unknowns.

5. Certain factors resist quantification. Basically, these are items which depend upon human relations. We have all seen dramatic improvements in factory production, sales, and even research brought about by improved human relations at both lower and higher levels of management. To put human relations skills into an MIS system is most difficult.

This is surely not to dismiss MIS. On the contrary, it is one of the secrets of a successful operation. But MIS must be individually developed to fit the manager's needs and bolster him in areas in which he may be weak. It cannot be a pat, canned approach. But neither can it be a matter of asking the manager what he needs and giving it to him, because he often does not know what he needs.

In a one-man shop, the manager, typically, records:

Cash, from day to day
Backlog of sales orders
Materials on hand and on order
Production
Sales

Accordingly, he is pretty well on top of the situation and has most facts at hand on which to base reasoned judgments.

As his business expands, however, he must depend on others to observe, measure, and record, and to communicate these measurements to him, either verbally or in writing. It is at this point that MIS comes into the picture.

Every business and every function of a business needs MIS. Four main problem areas of a typical business are the following:

1. *Marketing* (the prime source of revenues in most cases)
   a. How did we do?
      What were our sales by product, customer, and salesman and how did they compare to our planned sales?
      What were our sales as a share of the market, compared to our competition?
   b. What should we expect?
      What is the backlog of sales orders?
      What are the trends of the population and its buying habits?
2. *Production*
   a. How did we do?
      What were the costs per product compared to what we expected?
   b. What should we expect?
      Are costs going up or down, and why?
3. *Finance*
   a. Where do we stand?
      How are we doing on collection of receivables?
      Can we pay our bills? What is the cash on hand?
   b. What do we expect?
      How much money will we need in the future and where will we get it?
      What are the trends in the money market which might guide us to best solutions?
4. *Research and Development*
   a. How did we do?

What concrete accomplishments have been made? Why and at what costs?

b. Where should future efforts be pointed?

How should we invest future monies to produce the best results?

This outline of some of the major problems of a business indicates some areas of management decision making in which MIS can help. Obviously, in many of these areas Operations Research can be helpful in guiding decision making, but only if the facts on what has happened and is likely to happen (MIS) are available.

Of course, the art of communication enters into any MIS. The information being transmitted must be understood as easily and quickly as possible. Earlier, we envisioned the busy executive up to his hips in paper. Can you imagine trying to read the *New York Times* or the *Wall Street Journal* without titles, subheadings, or summaries of important articles? The fact that "it's all there" is hardly a comfort to the busy executive.

The breadth and level of detail of information given to the manager must be limited, and he should receive information only about those activities for which he is responsible. For example, the salesman does not need current production information, but he does need data on deliveries of the product he is selling. The president does not need details of what is happening on the production line. He does need enough information to monitor major problems in production.

Also, all executives need an information system which will flag all major items that are not going according to plan (see Management by Exception in Chapter 3).

In the future, well-constructed Management Information Systems will become increasingly important for the following reasons:

1. The complexity and magnitude of business operations will continue to grow.

2. The ability of management to use more information (more intelligent managers) will increase.

3. There will be growing use of specialists for specific problems

to be solved by Operations Research and othe ods, and better facts must be available for them.

4. The ability to store and manipulate inform its rapid growth. For example, in the last decad putation have decreased by 100 to 1; costs of s creased 1,000 to 1; and speed has increased 1,00 look forward to the time when all pertinent facts ab will be stored in a computer, ready to pop out as asked reasonable price.

5. Long-distance transmission of information is rapi ing faster and cheaper.

6. The ability to communicate is improving very fas facts can be presented in increasingly more relevant formats

One final word—do not construct an MIS based upon the manager what he wants. He has been tied down too l restraints on availability of information. Instead, tell him w can have.

Summary

It might seem that the greater the amount of factual informatio available, the wiser management decisions become. Unfortunately this is not true, and many a manager is so bogged down in a morass of computer runs that he cannot distinguish important facts from insignificant ones.

A well-constructed MIS system is based upon the knowledge of what information is available, the cost of accumulating, storing and retrieving such information, and the relative importance of the various items of information in arriving at valid management decisions.

Each level of management has different information requirements. If operations are going according to plan, a minimum of information is needed on a day-to-day basis. When things are not going according to plan, a "red flag" should be raised as quickly as possible.

PART II

Management Uses of Accounting

5 The Uses and Limitations of Conventional Accounting Statements

Traditionally, most businesses rely upon two statements—the balance sheet and the profit and loss statement—to tell them where they stand and how well they have done. An examination of what can be gained from these statements, and wherein the pitfalls lie, can be useful in setting up a program for planning and controlling profits.

Accounting is not an absolute science, in which all decisions are made in terms of black versus white. Given an agreed-upon factual situation, varying accounting techniques could be used which would produce markedly different results. In brief, much of accounting is an art.

The Balance Sheet

The typical use of the balance sheet has been to determine where a company stands at a given time. Although this function is a valid one, the balance sheet can be even more useful in planning for the future, particularly if its limitations are recognized. The very term, *balance sheet,* is somewhat anachronistic in that it stresses the seemingly magic balancing between assets and liabilities.

In actuality, the balance sheet is composed not of two parts, but of three: assets, liabilities, and owner's or stockholders' equity. It balances, not by use of mirrors, but because assets (what one owns) less liabilities (what one owes) must equal owner's or stockholders' equity (net ownership).

A more descriptive term for a balance sheet is *statement of financial position,* in that it is a snapshot of how a business stands at a given time. It does not purport to express what has happened over any particular period of time, but rather sets forth where a company is at a certain moment. In this sense, it is a still picture as compared to a profit and loss statement, which is a moving one.

Most confusion over the use of a balance sheet arises from the fact that values are expressed in terms of cost or market, whichever is lower. In recent years, the changing value of the dollar has made balance sheets a combination of present and past values, which make such figures as total assets virtually meaningless, whether considered in terms of liquidation values or any other standard. To illustrate the limitations of relying on balance sheet values in assessing the worth of company: if an oil company makes a major strike, increasing its real worth markedly, its balance sheet might be little changed. Let us look now at the items on a typical balance sheet.

Assets

Assets are traditionally subdivided into two groups, current and other. *Current assets* are those which, in the normal course of business, will be readily and quickly realized. *Other assets* are those which will be realized over a longer period.

In the category of current assets are cash, accounts receivable (assuming appropriate bad debt allowances), and prepaid expenses. These leave little room for argument in that they must be stated in no uncertain terms. Marketable securities, however, even when considered a current asset in which cash is invested on a "turnaround" basis, are traditionally stated at cost. Thus, balance sheet figures for these may have little relation to current values. The listing for inventories, depending on whether FIFO (first-in, first-out), LIFO (last-in, first-out—both will be described later in this chapter), or some other method is used, may be near current market or far less.

Other assets include land, buildings, machinery and equipment, patterns, dies, drawings and plates, long-term investments, and intangibles. All are stated at cost less amortization or depreciation, where applicable. Here balance sheets, if interpreted as indicative of realizable values, can be most misleading. For example: a well-known brewing company bought a parcel of land in 1913 for $1,360,000. This land is still carried on the balance sheet at this cost, although current appraised value approximates $25,000,000. Another question in this field—what value attaches to a trademark? All too often it does not even appear on the balance sheets. It should be clear, then, that assets, as stated on the balance sheet, are not necessarily representative of realizable values.

Liabilities

Liabilities, on the other hand, are fairly definite and determinable. Whether current or long-term debt, they represent specific claims against the company, and should be definitely stated. In viewing liabilities, the big area in question is contingencies. How real is a tax claim pressed by the government? What are the potentials involved in pending law suits? Such questions, in some cases almost imponderable, may have great bearing on the stated financial position of a company.

Owner's Equity

The owner's or *stockholders' equity* portion of a balance sheet (sometimes called net worth or book value) may be exceedingly complicated, but, in reality, it represents what is left after subtracting liabilities from assets. The "book value" of a stock is often virtually meaningless.

Recently the New York Stock Exchange reported an analysis of the 1,055 common stocks listed on the big board. At that time, 660 stocks were selling above book value and 395 below book value. There were wide variations: 202 stocks were selling at 100 per cent or more above book value, and 72 were selling for 50 per cent of book value or less.

TABLE 5–1

COMPANY A
Balance Sheet
December 31
(In thousands)

Assets

Current Assets		
Cash	$ 5,511	
U.S. gov't. securities at cost	1,756	
Accounts receivable	16,170	
Inventories—at lower of cost or market	34,014	
Prepaid expenses	4,975	
Total current assets		$ 62,426
Fixed Assets		
Property, plant, and equipment	$63,607	
Less: accumulated depreciation	23,024	40,583
Patents, good will, etc.		6,344
Total Assets		$109,353

Liabilities and Stockholders' Equity

Current Liabilities		
Accounts payable	$ 5,899	
Accrued expenses	8,559	
Other current liabilities	2,717	
Total current liabilities		$ 17,175
Mortgages, notes, and debentures		33,778
Stockholders' Equity		
Capital stock		
Common—2,391,500 shares issued	$ 5,853	
Capital surplus	35,870	
Earned surplus	16,677	
Total stockholders' equity		58,400
Total Liabilities and Stockholders' Equity		$109,353
Stockholders' equity per share of common stock		$24.42

From the summary balance sheets shown in Tables 5–1 and 5–2, it may look as though a share of Company A common stock is worth about the same as a share of Company B common stock.

TABLE 5–2

COMPANY B
Balance Sheet
December 31
(In thousands)

Assets

Current Assets		
Cash	$10,588	
Marketable securities	1,602	
Accounts receivable	28,081	
Inventories—at lower of cost or market	60,961	
Prepaid expenses	1,253	
Total current assets		$102,485
Fixed Assets		
Property, plant, and equipment at cost	$21,018	
Less: accumulated depreciation	10,775	
		10,243
Patents, licenses, developments, good will, etc.	$3,232	
Less: amortization to date	1,472	
		1,760
Total Assets		$114,488

Liabilities and Stockholders' Equity

Current Liabilities		
Accounts payable and accrued liabilities	$10,126	
Current maturities on long-term debt	3,484	
Federal, state, and other taxes	3,884	
Total current liabilities		$ 17,494
Long-term debt		46,829
Deferred federal income taxes		3,530
Stockholders' Equity		
Capital stock		
Common—1,865,000 shares issued	$15,872	
Capital surplus	18,453	
Earned surplus	12,310	
Total capital		46,635
Total Liabilities and Stockholders' Equity		$114,488
Stockholders' equity per share of common stock		$25.01

Each has approximately the same book value (total stockholders' equity divided by number of shares outstanding). In actuality, shares of Company A stock are selling at about four times the current price of shares of Company B stock. Since the balance sheet of any company cannot be viewed in a vacuum, let us look at the general area of profit and loss statements to find why such a wide variation in price of shares should exist.

The Profit and Loss Statement

Unlike a balance sheet, a profit and loss statement views an enterprise over a period of time, and it reflects results achieved over that period. Accountants prefer the term "income statement" primarily because of its brevity. Here we see an example of one of the major problems in interpreting accounting to the layman—semantics. Webster defines income as "that gain or recurrent benefit (usually measured in money) which proceeds from labor, business, or property; revenue; receipts." The accountant must be much more precise. In the broad sense, income is what a business takes in, but most accountants term the gross intake as "revenues" and reserve the term "income" for what is left after costs and expenses have been deducted.

Typically, the income, or profit and loss, statement is composed of four major elements: revenues; cost of goods sold; selling, general, and administrative expenses; and income taxes.

Revenues

Reporting of *revenues* is generally fairly straightforward, although practices differ in such areas as handling of discounts and commissions and the realizing of installment sales.

Cost of Goods Sold

The *cost of goods sold* category is the one in which the widest variations in practices are found, even within an industry. Typically, cost of goods sold is computed by the following simple formula:

Amount of inventory on hand at beginning of period	$xxxx
Add: Purchases during period	xxxx
Production costs during period	xxxx
	$xxxx
Less: Amount of inventory on hand at end of period	xxxx
Cost of goods sold during period	$xxxx

Despite this straightforward formula, accounting techniques may result in widely varying results. Among the areas of greatest potential variance are the following:

What is the value of inventory at any given time? The general principle is that it should be stated at cost or market, whichever is lower, but this leaves a lot of leeway. Some companies use LIFO (last-in, first-out), which assumes that, for costing purposes, the last items purchased or manufactured are the first ones sold. In a period of generally rising prices, this procedure may result in inventories being stated at a fraction of current cost. Other companies use FIFO (first-in, first-out), which assumes for costing purposes that the goods in inventory longest are the first sold. Once again, in a period of rising prices, goods bought at lower prices are replaced at much higher prices; higher profits are reported, but inventories are stated higher.

How are production costs calculated? Several alternative depreciation rates are now available for the same types of equipment. The higher the depreciation rate in the early years, the greater will be the cost of goods sold for the period. On the other hand, when this happens, the balance sheet may be stated well below realizable value.

What, for purposes of evaluation, is "good" inventory? The inventory count and cost can often be calculated, but, when valuing at cost or market, whichever is lower, market value is virtually undeterminable. What are the jigs and dies worth, for example, for a commercial airplane which the manufacturer *hopes* he will sell? The problems of evaluation of inventory, where no ready market value can be established, can be extremely complex. Moreover, management has the option of considering research and development costs as expenses when incurred or of capitalizing them as assets on the balance sheet to be amortized as expenses in future years.

Expenses

Selling, general, and administrative expenses are rarely a matter of dispute, although advertising expenses, for example, in one year may benefit the next year's sales, rather than the year in which they were spent.

Taxes

Income taxes, in the past, represented the actual amount payable for the year. Recently, however, there has been a trend toward recognizing future tax effects of what is being done currently. Although this approach has great merit, it means that no longer do income tax figures on an annual statement directly reflect what any given company will have to pay for the period covered by the statement. And the fact that, in some cases, accounting for statement purposes and for tax purposes may vary can further confuse the picture.

Over-all Effects

Admittedly, in presenting our examples, we have "stacked the deck" by not including the "notes to financial statements" which are an integral part of the statements. But if we temporarily ignore the notes to financial statements, we see the comparative profit and loss statement shown in Table 5–3.

Here we see that Company B reported a net income per share slightly higher than Company A. This fact, coupled with the stockholders' equity figure shown in Tables 5–1 and 5–2, would tend to make a person unused to reading financial statements believe that the two stocks should have approximately the same value.

TABLE 5–3

COMPANIES A AND B
Comparative Profit and Loss Statements
Year ended December 31
(In thousands)

	A	B
Revenues	$141,876	$154,100
Cost of sales		
Cost of sales and operating expenses	$ 91,086	$121,367
Depreciation and amortization	8,042	2,127
	$ 99,128	$123,494
Gross profit on sales	$ 42,748	$ 30,606
Selling, advertising, and administrative expense	20,958	18,495
Profit from operations	$ 21,790	$ 12,111
Other income	959	2,018
	$ 22,749	$ 14,129
Other charges	2,519	5,479
Income before federal income taxes	$ 20,230	$ 8,650
Provision for federal income taxes	10,707	327
Net income	$ 9,523	$ 8,323
Net income per share of common stock	$3.97	$4.46

Now let us turn to the "notes to financial statements," for they may well shed further light on the situation.

Inventories. Company A uses the LIFO method of evaluating inventories, while Company B uses the FIFO method. Company A's inventories have a current market value of about three times stated cost (Table 5–1). If this were reflected in the balance sheet, it would result in doubling stockholders' equity per share. Company B's inventories are stated at approximate current market.

Depreciation. Company A has invested in new, more efficient equipment in recent years and has elected to depreciate this equipment by the "declining balance" method, which results in higher depreciation charges against earnings in the early years and compensatingly lower charges in later years. Company B has made no major equipment acquisitions for ten years.

Taxes. Company A calculated its income taxes at the regular rate based on income for this particular year. Since Company B had operated at a loss in two preceding years, the carry forward of this loss reduced its taxes for the year in question to a nominal amount. Had the full tax rate been applicable, its profit per share would have been about one-half of what was reported.

This is an extreme example, but it encompasses only three of the many possibilities of varying accounting treatments of business situations. The fact that Company A has a substantially higher gross profit margin than Company B in the face of higher depreciation charges and higher reported materials costs (because of using LIFO) alone makes Company A stock worth considerably more than that of Company B. Viewed in this light, plus the temporary tax break that Company B has, it is easy to see why Company A's stock is selling for four times the price of Company B's stock.

Where accounting principles are consistently applied, much can be learned from studying comparable statements. But companies, even in the same business, can rarely be compared without a detailed understanding of what their figures really mean. Moreover, although a study of what has happened in the past may be of both interest and help, management gains most from looking ahead, not backward. The past can be of help in plotting the future, but only if it is used as a foundation, with future building planned on new conditions.

One other traditional statement occasionally used may be of considerable value to management planning—the statement of source and application of funds.

The Statement of Source and Application of Funds

A major problem in many businesses is "How do we stand for cash?" Neither the balance sheet nor the earnings statement shows what has happened to cash. Profits may result in more or less cash than you started with. At the same time, a business must watch its cash balance, and, no matter how profitable, cannot exist without cash to meet its obligations.

TABLE 5–4
STATEMENT OF SOURCES AND APPLICATIONS OF FUNDS

Sources of Funds

Net income	$10,000	
Intangible development costs, depreciation, depletion, etc.	87,000	
Increase in long-term debt—net	31,000	
Other transactions	11,000	
Total funds available		$139,000

Funds Applied to

Increase in plant and property	$18,000	
Investments in subsidiaries and other companies	5,000	
Dividends paid to stockholders	12,000	
Total funds used		35,000
Net increase in cash and securities		$104,000

Table 5–4 is a "where-got-where-gone" statement which reflects what happened to cash in a small oil company that showed a profit of only $10,000 on its earnings statement last year.

Cash was increased over the year by $104,000, while reported profits were only $10,000. Although this fact is of great historical interest, the real lesson to be learned is how this sort of study can be helpful in future planning. It should be obvious that the management of a small company might make far different future plans if it anticipated $100,000 cash to be generated from its enterprise than if it expected available cash to be limited to anticipated profits —in this case $10,000.

In discussing the balance sheet, the earnings statement, and the statement of source and application of funds, I do not mean to deprecate them. Although they have value as historical representations, they can be most helpful if properly used in looking at the future. Past results should be considered, but future plans should recognize ever-changing conditions in our dynamic society. Moreover, reported results depend, to a major extent, on the accounting concepts employed. Accountants, as a professional group, are disturbed about some of the wide variations in concepts and techniques now used, and are taking steps to close some of the gaps. Let us, then, take a brief look at some of the major problems facing the profession.

The Interpretation of Financial Statements: Ratio Analysis

Ratio analysis is the study of the relationship between the major components of financial statements. This technique is used extensively by creditors, investors, security analysts, and corporate personnel in assessing a company's financial position. By looking at ratios instead of absolute numbers, companies (or divisions) of different sizes can be easily compared. This assumes, of course, that similar accounting techniques are employed.

We shall discuss only a few of the most important ratios. Depending on the needs of management, other ratios may be useful.

A widely used measure of liquidity is the *current ratio*. This ratio is an attempt to estimate the ability of a business to meet its current obligations. It is computed by dividing current assets (cash, marketable securities, accounts receivable, inventory, prepaid expenses) by current liabilities (accounts payable, accrued taxes, expenses, currently maturing debts or notes). The balance sheet of Company A (Table 5–1) shows liabilities of $17,175,000 due in the current year. As of December 31, there was $62,426,000 in current assets to meet these obligations. Thus, the current ratio is 62426/17175, or 3:64. This compares favorably with the generally accepted rule-of-thumb figure of 2.00.

The major defect of the current ratio is that it assumes all current assets are liquid, that is, that they can be converted into cash quickly and without major loss. But in the case of inventory and prepaid expenses, this may not be true. Therefore, many companies use what is commonly referred to as the *quick ratio* (or acid test) to measure liquidity. In this ratio, inventories and prepaid expenses are deducted from current assets and the remainder is divided by current liabilities. A general rule of thumb is that a 1:1 ratio is satisfactory. For Company A, the ratio is 23437/17175, or 1:37.

A word of caution about use of the "rule of thumb": Some people tend to evaluate companies by use of ratios and rule-of-thumb figures without looking at the underlying facts. Many companies with a quick ratio of $\frac{1}{2}$ to 1 or less are doing extremely well; others with a quick ratio of over 4 to 1 are headed for bankruptcy. In short, while ratios can be helpful in analyzing a company, they are useful only to the extent that the analyst understands the make-up of the underlying figures.

A debt-to-equity ratio measures the degree of risk in a company. Generally, the greater the stockholders' equity in relation to debt, the greater the protection to the creditors. However, judicious use of debt financing can increase returns to stockholders. For example, if the company's investments earn 10 per cent and the interest on borrowed money for the investment is only 8 per cent, the 2 per cent differential accrues to the stockholder. In the above example, the "leverage" is favorable. Conversely, leverage may be unfavorable if return on investment is less than interest on debt. It is a common maxim that the greater the amount of debt financing, the greater the risk. Although there is much variation between industries, a frequently quoted, but relatively meaningless, rule of thumb is that there should be equal amounts of debt and equity. In our example, the debt equity ratio of Company A is a conservative 0.87. The stockholder might be far better off, in a growth situation for example, to have a debt equity ratio of 5 to 1 or more.

Another useful measure is the *net-sales-to-inventory ratio.* As we shall see, the costs of carrying inventory can be great. This ratio is an indication of whether a company is carrying excessive inventories in relation to sales. As a practical matter, since inventory levels are changing throughout the year, some average inventory figure should be used. Most commonly, an average of the beginning and ending inventories is used; if this is not representative, an average of monthly inventory levels should be used. For Company A (see Tables 5–3 and 5–1), we find a sales-to-inventory ratio of 141876/34014, or 4.16.

This ratio is sometimes called the *inventory turnover.* In general, the higher it is, the better for profits, but companies manufacturing for specific orders may have a very low net sales inventory ratio and still do very well.

Two measures are helpful in analysis of the profitability of the firm. The return on sales shows the net profit per dollar of sales. Either a before- or after-tax profit figure can be used. But if we are comparing companies with different tax rates or the same company with tax rates changing over the years examined, a before-tax measure may be better. For Company A, the return on sales (on an after-tax basis) is 6.7 per cent. A second ratio, *net profit/stockholders' equity,* measures the return on the stockholders' investment in the firm. Here, an after-tax figure is most commonly used. This information is used by shareholders to determine how their return compares with alternative investments. For Company A, the return on equity is 16.3 per cent, which compares favorably with a 10 per cent minimum under the accepted rule of thumb.

Throughout this discussion, we have referred to certain rules of thumb to use in evaluation. As Table 5–5 clearly shows, there are, in fact, major differences in ratio values between industries. For example, the median return on equity is 11.01 per cent in general industrial machinery and equipment companies, but only 6.08 per cent in fur goods. Comparative data can be useful in evaluating the ratios of a particular company. Dun & Bradstreet's *Key Business Ratios* is the most widely used source of comparative ratios of different industries. It computes 14 such ratios for 125 lines of business. Data on comparative ratios can also be found in *Statement Studies* published by Robert Morris Associates, the quarterly reports of the Federal Trade Commission and Securities and Exchange Commission, reports of the Accounting Corporation of America (mainly on smaller companies), and in various reports of trade associations. Furthermore, the comparison with similar ratios for the particular company in previous years can also be helpful.

Warning: Although ratio analysis can be a valuable tool in gaining insights into the operations of a business, it must be remembered that the ratios are merely products of the financial statements. Therefore, the reader should be aware that *all* the limitations of accounting statements discussed previously apply to ratio analysis.

TABLE 5-5

Manufacturing & Construction

Line of Business (and number of concerns reporting)	Current assets to current debt	Net profits on net sales	Net profits on tangible net worth	Net profits on net working capital	Net sales to tangible net worth	Net sales to net working capital	Collection period	Net sales to inventory	Fixed assets to tangible net worth	Current debt to tangible net worth	Total debt to tangible net worth	Inventory to net working capital	Current debt to inventory	Funded debts to net working capital
	Times	Per cent	Per cent	Per cent	Times	Times	Days	Times	Per cent	Per cent	Per cent	Per cent	Per cent	Per cent
3441-42-43-44-46-49 Fabricated Structural Metal Products (125)	4.29	4.82	15.44	23.13	4.16	7.11	41	9.8	20.6	23.2	46.2	48.6	59.8	11.7
	2.49	3.16	9.11	12.51	2.97	4.60	52	5.6	36.7	44.5	79.1	74.5	94.5	32.3
	1.58	1.55	4.58	6.26	2.18	3.10	69	4.1	57.3	87.7	132.2	116.9	141.2	62.3
3522 Farm Machinery & Equipment (71)	4.09	5.10	14.86	20.80	4.29	6.16	28	10.3	20.5	23.0	47.2	65.8	42.4	21.8
	2.50	2.86	8.47	14.60	2.81	3.58	44	3.7	34.2	50.1	87.7	97.1	64.8	39.0
	1.90	1.26	4.20	6.57	2.02	2.41	59	3.0	60.6	80.3	146.1	126.0	91.2	67.2
3141 Footwear (115)	3.66	4.18	16.21	21.93	5.87	8.62	35	7.3	12.5	31.3	46.5	66.0	52.2	7.9
	2.19	2.94	11.35	15.03	4.24	4.98	48	5.4	22.7	62.4	95.8	97.4	89.1	21.2
	1.54	1.59	7.16	9.71	2.96	3.51	61	3.9	37.5	129.0	171.1	157.0	133.0	42.2
2371 Fur Goods (54)	2.60	2.15	14.62	15.89	9.10	10.43	27	10.0	1.1	60.1	**	67.1	82.6	**
	1.76	1.04	6.08	6.21	5.58	6.47	42	6.7	3.2	117.5	**	105.5	125.8	**
	1.53	0.33	2.43	2.74	3.63	3.98	64	4.4	8.7	166.1	**	147.2	166.5	**
1511 General Building Contractors (192)	2.06	2.61	16.50	26.73	13.25	22.95	**	**	10.9	62.4	110.5	**	**	16.6
	1.49	1.31	10.33	16.20	8.01	12.55	**	**	25.9	129.2	203.5	**	**	38.1
	1.22	0.49	5.00	8.19	4.65	7.28	**	**	49.2	221.4	303.2	**	**	100.9
3561-62-64-65-66-67-69 Genl. Indus. Machy. & Equipment (106)	3.70	6.20	14.78	24.64	3.94	6.66	38	7.6	28.4	22.9	52.6	64.5	51.6	23.0
	2.61	4.13	11.01	17.42	2.92	4.24	51	4.8	44.8	42.2	83.1	83.4	81.8	43.1
	1.79	2.47	8.03	11.06	1.98	2.93	65	3.9	70.4	70.7	122.9	107.9	127.7	73.8
2041-42-43-44-45-46 Grain Mill Products (72)	3.71	3.06	13.29	31.37	5.82	15.98	19	19.5	31.3	18.6	33.3	49.7	67.0	19.5
	2.25	1.72	8.17	17.23	4.29	8.96	26	12.0	49.5	35.3	60.8	80.8	101.7	45.4
	1.57	0.91	4.51	8.37	3.17	5.76	34	8.6	70.8	67.7	104.1	119.9	142.8	67.9
3431-32-33 Heating Apparatus & Plumbing Fixtures (40)	4.42	4.83	11.73	15.73	3.47	5.20	36	6.7	16.3	22.4	39.7	53.5	52.8	17.5
	3.19	2.97	8.27	10.63	2.76	3.66	48	5.6	37.5	31.4	60.7	81.3	72.5	23.6
	2.03	1.94	5.68	7.30	1.87	3.09	62	4.4	49.8	59.6	88.4	97.8	100.0	47.2
1621 Heavy Construction, except Highway & Street (113)	3.17	4.64	16.42	36.35	6.37	12.07	**	**	31.2	24.3	52.7	**	**	11.3
	1.82	2.71	10.03	17.96	3.58	7.10	**	**	54.9	54.8	99.9	**	**	43.3
	1.37	1.01	5.27	8.61	2.19	3.86	**	**	75.8	105.4	152.8	**	**	108.0
2251-52 Hosiery (57)	4.04	4.30	13.95	24.10	4.58	7.48	34	8.2	30.3	18.8	47.9	62.5	56.4	26.2
	2.44	2.36	7.06	11.76	2.66	5.10	46	5.8	45.8	42.2	67.7	88.2	74.9	38.1
	1.79	1.39	3.41	7.25	1.87	3.44	62	3.4	70.0	85.3	133.6	118.5	106.9	75.8
3631-32-33-34-35-36-39 Household Appliances (43)	3.86	4.68	14.13	34.35	3.97	7.22	28	7.3	19.3	23.0	44.0	71.4	52.4	21.3
	2.57	3.16	10.99	14.50	2.90	4.50	41	5.1	36.1	41.8	85.2	89.0	75.1	36.1
	1.54	2.19	7.06	8.07	2.22	3.09	64	3.7	56.7	79.7	122.8	146.4	99.5	66.9
2812-13-15-16-18-19 Industrial Chemicals (59)	3.13	6.55	13.81	49.71	2.59	10.10	38	11.1	36.2	17.1	30.2	55.7	66.7	38.0
	2.05	4.65	10.34	23.45	1.88	5.19	51	7.4	54.1	29.5	52.6	68.0	100.0	95.8
	1.40	2.54	6.28	10.21	1.59	3.17	64	5.4	82.5	49.3	83.2	100.9	179.9	198.7
3821-22 Instruments, Measuring & Controlling (41)	3.97	5.90	15.19	20.20	3.41	4.29	44	5.5	26.1	22.1	41.3	60.2	51.3	15.8
	2.70	4.41	11.76	14.39	2.31	3.40	62	4.4	40.2	33.1	81.1	83.8	68.9	39.9
	2.00	3.11	6.98	7.93	1.82	2.54	75	3.4	58.3	69.1	123.3	93.4	101.6	62.7
3321-22-23 Iron & Steel Foundries (63)	4.03	4.57	13.77	27.02	3.13	8.45	33	21.4	42.0	19.0	38.0	30.2	84.7	22.0
	2.52	2.92	6.99	15.48	2.56	5.40	42	12.3	59.9	27.4	54.9	45.7	118.1	39.2
	1.85	1.41	3.71	6.91	1.89	3.84	52	6.0	71.8	40.5	97.4	87.7	203.8	67.4
2253 Knit Outerwear Mills (58)	2.37	4.80	16.67	25.21	7.42	11.35	25	9.5	3.6	53.6	68.8	75.1	71.2	24.3
	1.86	1.97	11.14	15.02	4.77	6.79	41	6.0	22.1	81.7	103.8	110.6	101.1	30.6
	1.48	1.29	8.08	9.95	3.49	4.55	63	4.3	44.9	138.2	167.1	161.5	142.2	54.9
2082 Malt Liquors (32)	3.19	4.67	11.94	50.29	3.51	20.10	8	23.4	54.2	17.5	29.9	33.8	110.9	32.3
	2.02	2.43	5.87	17.04	2.51	9.58	17	17.5	69.9	24.8	60.3	57.3	165.3	114.2
	1.52	(0.19)	(0.86)	(1.24)	1.91	5.87	27	11.5	87.7	35.1	81.0	109.0	231.0	263.7
2515 Mattresses & Bedsprings (44)	3.68	3.83	12.46	19.14	5.70	8.49	43	11.1	13.4	22.3	48.1	47.3	68.5	5.7
	2.31	2.19	7.58	11.34	3.35	5.23	51	8.4	23.4	46.5	73.3	70.2	99.3	22.9
	1.83	1.22	3.32	5.07	2.47	3.89	59	6.1	41.6	78.0	107.8	107.8	155.6	40.5
2011 Meat Packing Plants (92)	3.96	1.50	13.01	26.85	12.77	35.26	11	45.2	35.7	15.9	40.4	39.4	72.9	21.0
	2.52	0.73	6.80	14.87	9.52	17.98	12	30.0	54.8	37.8	81.6	61.8	100.0	59.2
	1.36	0.15	1.51	3.79	5.92	12.78	16	21.0	77.5	70.4	135.9	141.2	180.2	111.1
3461 Metal Stampings (100)	3.44	4.71	15.90	33.10	4.32	7.91	28	13.5	34.7	22.1	47.3	43.9	77.2	20.0
	2.41	3.59	10.68	20.61	3.07	5.47	35	9.3	50.1	35.4	80.5	69.4	106.5	33.5
	1.75	2.06	6.45	12.12	1.91	3.88	46	6.6	74.1	64.8	123.7	101.1	174.4	74.0
3541-42-44-45-48 Metalworking Machy. & Equipment (126)	4.05	6.78	13.54	27.03	3.09	6.16	35	13.9	33.6	19.5	43.3	46.9	50.9	19.2
	2.76	4.33	10.41	17.48	2.21	3.81	47	6.1	46.5	32.8	63.6	68.7	79.1	38.0
	1.81	2.34	5.73	8.87	1.68	2.76	61	3.6	63.8	58.7	115.3	97.7	175.8	71.6
2431 Millwork (37)	4.16	4.65	12.04	21.38	4.54	7.18	35	9.2	17.5	22.3	41.1	56.1	58.2	12.4
	2.56	2.36	7.29	12.53	3.49	4.89	45	6.8	31.3	33.7	83.3	75.1	90.5	33.6
	1.83	1.04	3.92	7.64	2.10	3.46	57	4.5	54.4	80.0	164.7	132.9	138.3	84.5
3599 Miscellaneous Machinery, except Electrical (91)	4.30	6.89	17.91	35.09	4.11	7.64	29	23.2	25.4	15.7	37.4	25.0	66.6	25.3
	2.59	4.27	10.30	19.25	2.61	5.28	41	9.1	48.2	32.0	74.5	54.8	104.5	56.9
	1.71	2.32	5.84	11.33	1.75	3.38	55	4.8	85.9	70.8	125.1	91.3	275.3	128.3
3714 Motor Vehicle Parts & Accessories (77)	3.84	6.40	17.40	33.70	3.43	6.23	35	9.3	23.8	23.5	49.3	58.8	52.9	27.7
	2.68	4.49	12.53	19.19	2.75	4.13	41	6.1	41.3	36.0	63.5	84.2	81.5	42.1
	2.13	2.95	7.23	9.94	2.13	3.19	50	4.1	54.8	52.6	117.2	98.2	103.5	89.3
3361-62-69 Nonferrous Foundries (47)	3.54	4.78	13.43	40.76	4.01	10.87	27	24.1	33.7	16.4	43.5	29.2	83.5	22.3
	2.48	3.03	7.69	19.67	2.60	5.35	39	13.0	50.1	34.1	54.9	62.8	144.9	27.2
	1.61	0.36	2.25	3.25	1.91	3.69	48	7.2	65.0	49.7	74.5	96.5	298.0	111.0

( ) Indicates loss.

** Not computed. Printers carry only current supplies such as paper, ink, and binding materials rather than merchandise inventories for re-sale. Building Trades contractors have no inventories in the credit sense of the term. As a general rule, such contractors have no customary selling terms, each contract being a special job for which individual terms are arranged. This sample included no manufacturers of fur goods with funded debts.

"Key Business Ratios" is reprinted from *Key Business Ratios* with the permission of the publisher, Dun & Bradstreet, Inc.

Changing Concepts of Accounting

Accounting, as most commonly used, represents an attempt to quantify, in dollars, what has happened in a business over a period of time. At first blush, it would seem easy to express both sales and expenses in dollars for any period and produce a balance sheet and a profit and loss statement which would leave no room for argument.

Accounting is not quite that simple. As pointed out earlier, it is a combination of both science and art, and there is room for debate in connection with a number of accounting principles. This fact need not cause any difficulties in planning and control so long as certain controversial areas are understood.

CHANGING PRICE LEVELS. Should financial statements be adjusted to give effect to price-level changes? Much of the difficulty here stems from depreciation problems. Most people will agree that the cost of an asset which will be useful for more than one year (a building, for example) should be spread over its useful life as a charge against income. CPAs as a group have long held that the purpose of depreciation is the recoupment of the purchase price of a wasting asset. But let management beware if it counts on replacing an asset from cash provided by depreciation over, say, the last twenty years. Further, the typical balance sheet now is a hodgepodge, with different assets purchased at different price levels. It expresses neither replacement value nor liquidation value. There is general agreement that this area is a problem, but no agreement as to what should be done about it.

TIMING OF REALIZATION OF INCOME. It is generally understood that income should be recognized when services are rendered or goods delivered, but business practice varies widely. In the case of some mining enterprises, income is reported at the time of production. At the other extreme, income is sometimes not recognized until cash is collected in some installment sales. With this wide variation, management must be sure of where it stands when it reviews its own or other companies' financial results.

BYPASSING THE EARNINGS STATEMENT. How should adjustments reflecting activities of prior years be handled? There is considerable room for variance in procedure. Sizable tax refunds, for example, may distort any one year's results.

ACCOUNTING FOR REGULATED INDUSTRIES. Some of the rulings made by regulatory commissions as to form and principles used in presenting financial information result in presentations which can be quite misleading, not only to stockholders and creditors but also to management itself.

INVENTORY VALUATIONS. As discussed on page 35 "first-in, first-out" (FIFO) and "last-in, first-out" (LIFO) are the two major approaches employed. Another method is the "weighted average," in which each time a new shipment of material is received, the price paid for the goods on hand is adjusted so that the new quantity reflects the average price paid for all goods in this category. This has the advantage of evening out fluctuations in price of materials.

In brief, varying methods of inventory valuations, which can produce widely different results, are available to like companies.

LOSS OF PRODUCTIVITY OF ASSETS. Suppose a motel on a busy highway finds itself bypassed by a turnpike, and business falls off sharply. There is no agreement as to when and how such a property should be devaluated. Or, suppose a new piece of equipment purchased or built turns out to be much less efficient than anticipated. Common sense would seem to dictate that a write-down in value is in order, but there are no established rules.

INCREASING USE OF LONG-TERM LEASES. As a side effect of "sale and long-term leaseback" arrangements, balance sheets normally do not record such contractual obligations as liabilities. This practice results in understating the liabilities of a company.

PENSION-PLAN LIABILITIES. Some companies set aside amounts designed to put pension funds on a full actuarial basis, including past service earned. Other companies charge only the amounts currently being paid to pensioned employees, with no balance sheet liability. Still others follow some in-between method. Differences in accounting treatment may, accordingly, lead to wide variations in reported figures on both the balance sheet and the earnings statement.

ACCOUNTING FOR RESEARCH AND DEVELOPMENT COSTS. Here, too, wide variations exist. Some companies expense all such items while others, with identical problems, capitalize them.

Many more variations in treatment could be cited, cloaked by the term "under generally accepted accounting principles." The point is that accounting is not cut and dried. The businessman must learn what his own figures mean, and not compare his operations with those of others without understanding that wide variations in techniques can and do exist.

Summary

The conventional accounting statements—balance sheet, profit and loss statement, and the statement of source and application of funds—have long been and will continue to be most important tools for both management and outsiders to use in gauging the condition of a business. Additional insight into the performance of the firm can be gained by using ratio analysis. As later chapters will show, however, these statements and ratios can be much more useful if used for plotting the future course of a business instead of merely reflecting past performance.

In viewing the various figures on financial statements, the footnotes to a statement must be considered an integral part of the statement. Failure to consider the additional facts set forth by footnotes may lead to erroneous conclusions.

Each item on the statements should be viewed as an entity. In most cases total assets, for example, is a meaningless figure reflecting cash at current dollar values, land at dollars paid years ago, and buildings and equipment at dollars paid at various times less depreciation, with results which may or may not have any relation to remaining useful value.

The balance sheet does not reflect liquidation values of an enterprise. Under forced sale, values obtainable might be considerably more or less. Neither does a balance sheet reflect replacement values, nor does it purport to.

Profit and loss statements for two firms of equal health doing the same amounts of business may show substantially different results, both in net income and in various items of revenues and costs.

Using conventional accounting statements intelligently requires detailed study of each item to ascertain what lies behind each of the figures presented.

6 Marketing

Although the significance of the marketing function varies among industries and even within a single industry, it is always of great importance. We hear of "production oriented" companies, and even "research oriented" companies, but manufacturing and research cannot produce profits in themselves. A profit is made only when an item is sold, and it is the marketing function that encompasses the movement of goods toward the consumer.

The marketing area is difficult to plan and control because it is the one area that has responsibility for forecasting and controlling *both* income and expenses. Moreover, consumer demand is probably the most difficult element of a budget to gauge.

Some years ago, the successful marketing executive was typically a great personal salesman. Today, he must be considerably more than that. He needs to use every bit of accounting information he can get, both in planning sales and in controlling the costs of his operations. He has to be on top of myriad reports, know what they signify, and be able to take quick corrective action.

The two major facets of the marketer's job are inextricably intertwined, but we shall consider them separately for the purpose of this chapter, taking up, first, problems in connection with sales revenues and, second, planning and control of distribution costs.

Sales Revenues

On the revenue side of the picture, the marketer is striving for the most profitable volume attainable. This means that he must aim not for maximum sales, but for maximum profits. Even though most elements of manufacturing costs (see Chapter 7) are outside his control, he must be aware of these costs and plan his operation so that he is selling the best possible amount of the right products at the best possible price.

The Sales Forecast

The sales forecast is of such paramount importance because upon it may be based heavy commitments in materials, peo, e, buildings, and equipment. It may lead to significant changes in research and development plans. It may, in fact, decidedly affect the morale of an entire organization. An accurate sales forecast, moreover, will make more economical operations possible in every phase of a business.

Preparing a good sales budget, although seemingly an exercise in magic, entails the full use of available facts for planning. The marketer must consider three major factors: (1) the business he feels sure of, based upon contracts or historical buying patterns; (2) the new business he expects to get or the old business he will lose because of some planned effort (for example, a promotion campaign on a certain product, addition of salesmen to open new markets, dropping of unprofitable products), and (3) matters outside his control (for example, cyclical demand for his product, changing consumer preferences).

Even to begin, a fair amount of statistical data must be assembled. The character of these data will, of course, depend upon the type of business in which a company is engaged. For example, the number of products you sell; your geographical distribution pattern; your customers, whether consumers or manufacturers; the type of product you sell, whether subject to wide fluctuations in demand or not; your policy decisions on dropping or adding products, expanding or restricting areas in which to sell—all these considerations affect the complexity of good sales budgeting procedure.

An Example of a Preliminary Sales Budget

Let us take the procedure followed by a well-known cosmetics company in preparing its yearly sales budget, using, for the sake of simplicity, only one product-line budget.

The ABC Cosmetics Company subscribes to certain national market-research services which indicate that the total market for Product D and its equivalent (expressed in manufacturer's prices) for the current year is in the neighborhood of $60 million. For the past four years, total market has been growing at the rate of 10 per cent per year, and every indication is that this rate of growth (about three times that of United States population growth) will continue in the following year.

The ABC Cosmetics Company's sales of Product D for the past three years expressed in thousands of dollars are shown in Table 6–1.

TABLE 6–1

Year	Sales to Normal Channels	Private Brand Sales	Total Sales
3d preceding	$12,500	$2,500	$15,000
2d preceding	15,000	3,000	18,000
1st preceding	18,000	3,000	21,000

The growth of sales through normal channels, which has averaged 20 per cent per year (twice the rate of total market growth), has been achieved largely by planned geographical expansion of the sales force, thus tapping new markets. At the end of the current year near-saturation coverage had been reached.

Private-brand sales, which were under contract with a large variety chain, have been less profitable each year. ABC Company is not unhappy that a competitor has underbid it and these sales will not exist in the following year.

From what is generally known in the trade, the plans of ABC's competitors for advertising and promotion of Product D are consistent with what they have done in preceding years.

After checking with his salesmen, the regional sales director for the newest geographical territory states that, although current year sales will amount to $2 million, sales for the last quarter (at which point full coverage of the territory had been reached) will be at the rate of $4 million per year.

A preliminary cast-up of these facts reveals that ABC Cosmetics Company, if it retains its share of the total market for the coming year, should have $22 million in sales of Product D ($18 million in the current year plus $2 million in annual rate in the new geographical region plus 10 per cent in total market, or $2 million). When this $22 million sales figure is put into preliminary budget profit and loss form, it indicates a net profit of $3 million for Product D. Since the ABC management has indicated it will be satisfied with a 20 per cent return on $12.5 million investment in Product D facilities the preliminary budget seems in line.

The foregoing example is not intended to be all-inclusive, but to indicate the use of accounting that goes into the preliminary forecasting process. Most actual preliminary budgets are not nearly this simple in construction nor so happy in immediate results.

Possible Problem Areas

Let us assume that projected sales are greater than the total productive facilities of the company involved. Some of the more obvious answers to this problem are these: add to the productive facilities, raise prices, or contract with outsiders to do some of the production. This is a nice kind of problem to have, but far better that it arise well before the events occur so that plans can be made to fill the gap to the best advantage of the company. From this example we can see at once the benefits to be derived from forward planning through a budget.

Suppose, on the other hand, that projected sales are not up to expectation and do not seem likely to produce the desired profit. This may prompt a hard look at the channels of distribution being used for the product. In general, depending upon the type of product involved, sales are made through wholesalers, through retailers, or to individual customers who actually use the product. Sales may be made on behalf of the company by salesmen on the company's payroll, by brokers, or by manufacturer's representatives. The latter may receive between 5 and 15 per cent of the sales price of the product.

Two basic considerations in determining the type of distribution you will want to have are: (1) How can you get the most efficient distribution of your product? (2) At what cost? For some years Chesebrough Manufacturing Company, makers of Vaseline and allied products, sold these products through Colgate Palmolive Company on a commission basis. Cost studies at varying levels of production indicated clearly that in this manner Chesebrough could get better coverage at less cost than if it had its own salesmen. At the same time company management recognized that it was handicapped by being the number two line in the enormous Colgate stable. One reason for the merger of Chesebrough with Ponds Extract Company without doubt, was that Ponds had its own nationwide sales force. As a result of the merger, Chesebrough thereby achieved lower costs and had more control over its salesmen.

Another consideration for management at this point is the alignment of sales territories, whether manufacturer's representatives are used or company salesmen. Statistics are available from both government and trade sources which, judiciously applied to any business, can indicate where a good sales job is or is not being done. A poor job may stem from lack of sales effort or from inefficient sales effort. Management must then determine whether the solution is adding more salesmen, realigning sales territories, or making some other move.

A related consideration is the continuation of nonprofitable departments or products. The fact that a part or a product is not profitable cannot be the sole consideration in deciding whether to continue production and sales. In some cases it is essential that a "full line" be carried; hence, losses on a certain product must be taken in order that the salesman may have a complete line to sell the customer. The point is that nonprofitable products should be dispensed with unless there is some real reason for keeping them. At any rate, you should know what your nonprofitable products are. Ways of determining which products are profitable are discussed in Chapter 7.

Analysis of accounting data on credit losses can also be very helpful. All too often, credit managers point with great pride to infinitesimally low credit losses. If credit losses are virtually nonexistent, it may mean that credit policy has been so restrictive that potential markets have been turned away. Only detailed analysis can determine whether too restrictive a policy has been followed.

Final Budget Preparation

Once again we get back to the fact that the preparation of a budget as a tool for planning and control of profits is one long continuous "cut-and-fit" process. As certain sales facts are determined, for example, production and research decisions may be influenced. The decisions made in production and research, in turn, have an impact on the sales picture.

Once the preliminary policy decisions have been made, construction of the detailed sales budget can begin. Each salesman is asked what he expects to sell, by product line, type of customer, and geographical location. These estimates go to the area manager, who evaluates, changes, and consolidates the forecasts. He then forwards his results to his superior, and so on, up the line. Each salesman and supervisor should consider the factors previously discussed in making his estimates.

The sales manager, in turn, must consider who on his staff are optimistic and tend to overestimate what they can do. He must also recognize that some of his people tend to set low budgets so that they can make heroes of themselves by beating their quotas. In addition he may have information which is not available to his subordinates and which may cause him to make changes in the figures presented. As a result of census figures or reports on what his competition is doing, he may decide to realign his sales force.

At this point, the knowledgeable budget director can be of great help to the chief executive officer by pointing out where, based on his experience and understanding of the problems, the budget is unrealistic, and suggesting changes. The sales manager, for example, may have shown in the past that he prefers budgets he is sure he can beat. Or, he may have a blind spot with reference to a specific product. Or, he may have assumed more favorable delivery dates than are possible. The budget director exerts what influence he can with the sales manager to get him to adjust his forecasts. If he is unsuccessful, he presents his facts to the chief executive officer.

We have now arrived at a sales budget—by product, geographically, in units to be sold, and dollar sales. At this point, top management takes another hard look at the assembled figures.

If the so-called "final" budget does not produce a profit that is satisfactory to management, a re-examination of all the facts and figures is in order, and fairly sweeping decisions may have to be made. Promotion plans may be shaved. New-product introductions (almost always costly) may be postponed. In effect, the whole budget will be gone over with a fine tooth comb at top-management level.

⌐ Price Setting

Pricing is, of course, a major factor in planning and controlling the profits of a business. Although pricing must be dynamic and subject to change as business conditions change, most basic decisions on pricing can and should be made as a part of the budgetary process. Many problems can thereby be solved before they actually arise. As part of the planning process, "ground rules" should be laid down so that salesmen, sales managers, and others on up the line know clearly how much discretion they have when they get out on the firing line. Many an order has been lost because of the length of time it took to get a decision from the home office.

Nevertheless, no single area of business seems to use less reasoning than does price setting. In price setting, the role of the man in charge of marketing varies from company to company, but almost always he plays a relatively major part. At the very least, he has some control over rebates, discounts, and quantity "deals." At the other extreme, he may control the whole price structure of the company.

We mentioned earlier that any sales budget should be prepared by product with both quantities and dollars. If quantities are left out, a management may be lulled into a false security; continual rises in dollar volume may merely reflect rising price levels while quantities and share of the market may be going down.

Prices are set either by what competition is charging, by what a company feels it can get, or by some preconception of a desired level of profit. Many decisions are made somewhere between these extreme viewpoints. But all too seldom does the detailed examination of costs play a major role in setting prices.

We are not so naive as to assume that many firms can compute their costs, apply a desired markup, and thereby set their prices across the board. What competition is doing must have influence on any company's price structure. On the other hand, if you know costs and markups on all your products, decisions on bringing out new products and dropping old ones become much clearer. Salesmen can then be motivated to promote the products with the higher markups.

Another major determinant in the pricing structure is anticipated volume at varying price levels. A marketing director might well produce a budget for sales of products at varying price levels. We have seen (page 12) that after the break-even point is passed, profits rise markedly. A sharp increase in sales volume for a product at a lower unit price may result in higher profits than the sale of fewer units at a higher price.

Without discussing varying rebate and discount policies in detail, let us note that companies subject to the Federal Trade Commission must be able to support any varying practices in these areas with specific cost data.

Distribution Costs

Costs of distribution break down into three major elements: direct selling expenses, advertising and promotion, and physical distribution expenses. Although each of these areas influences the others, we shall look at each separately.

Direct Selling Expenses

These expenses include all costs of obtaining orders, as opposed to general promotion and handling and delivery costs. Although a few companies rely completely on mail orders as a source of sales, direct selling expenses more typically consist of salespeople's compensation and expenses.

Planning and controlling salesmen's compensation and expenses is relatively easy, once management policies have been established. Establishing these policies, however, is a basic planning job which takes a lot of top attention.

In the first place, the job of the salesman should be analyzed to determine what specific skills it requires. Many so-called salesmen, for example, are nothing more than order-takers. On the other end of the scale are the qualified salesmen whose success or failure depends on a high degree of ingenuity and technical competence.

In the case of the "order-taker," it is characteristic that revenues produced are of a highly repetitive nature. Where this is true, accounting techniques can be used to determine what should be expected from each salesperson and how many salespeople should be employed to obtain the desired coverage of a market. In the case of a grocery salesman, for example, figures can be developed for costs per (1) dollar of net sales, (2) unit of product sold, (3) dollar of gross profit, (4) sales transaction, and (5) customers served. Examination of such statistics may lead to major changes in the dispersal of the sales force to gain maximum profits.

In one baking company, for example, analyses of the sales statistics revealed that 20 per cent of the routemen were calling on small isolated customers. The total sales of these routemen were less than the total costs of their salaries, commissions, and expenses. This kind of situation may be desirable when breaking into new territory, if the potential for the territory merits it. But companies often do not examine the coverage they are getting from their salesmen. As a result, one salesman who is giving his utmost and doing a good job may be badly underpaid based on his results. Another salesman may not be overexerting himself, but because of the chance distribution of customers within his territory, he may be making out very well financially.

In brief, where only repetitive selling or order-taking is required, the use of accounting control techniques is fairly simple and straightforward. By use of a market analysis, the sales potential for any given area can be established. Job standards can then be set for each salesperson, in which a standard time can be established for each call and mileage between calls. Standard frequencies for calls can also be established. When all this is done, salesmen's territories can be reasonably defined. The whole arrangement can be supervised by the use of call reports and data on sales obtained.

Not all selling situations are this simple. Where real creativeness is involved, as in much sales engineer work, the problem is more complex. For example, should salesmen be assigned geographically or by types of customer? Only examination of a company's particular situation, including the need for specialized knowledge in selling to specific industries, can be used to determine the answer here.

At the same time, the use of available accounting facts can make the salesman's job, and what is to be expected of him, a matter of objective judgment rather than subjective.

Once the salesman's job has been analyzed, the question of putting a price tag on it may be fairly complicated. An immediate question is whether some form of incentive compensation is desirable. In most cases, salesmen's compensation plans have been found to be most effective if some form of incentive payment is included. Table 6–2 shows the broad range of compensation methods used in business today.

Note that almost 90 per cent of the compensation plans shown in Table 6–2 include some sort of bonus or commission payment.

Most incentive compensation plans for salesmen are geared to net sales produced by the individual. Obviously, plans drawn up on that basis should not be used where the individual salesman is in a position to influence prices. In one major textile company, the sales manager of a product line which lost money for the year made more money that year than the president of the company by selling below cost. His contract called for a percentage of net sales; yet he had broad authority for price setting.

Incentive compensation plans range from the arbitrary awards of round sums to extremely detailed formulas. Many of the more progressive companies offer varying percentage bonuses on sales, with higher bonuses being paid for sales of products having higher profit margins. Rarely does an incentive bonus bring about real incentive unless it amounts to 30 per cent or more of salary. To provide real incentive, the bonus award must be made in some tangible form. There is nothing like hard cash paid as often as

TABLE 6–2

A. COMPENSATION METHODS BY INDUSTRY

Industry	Salary Plan	Commission Plan	Combination Plan
Advertising	—	50	50
Appliances, plumbing, heating	5	41	54
Autos, trucks, parts, etc.	—	44	56
Building construction	16	11	73
Chemical, petroleum, rubber	41	12	47
Drugs, cosmetics, pharmaceuticals	—	24	76
Electrical, electronics	18	21	61
Equipment—machines (nonelectrical)	9	9	82
Farm equipment, supplies, feed	10	20	70
Food, beverage	10	21	69
Hardware, tools	8	14	78
Housewares, furnishings	11	42	47
Insurance, mutuals	8	50	42
Primary metals, fabricators	22	—	78
School, office equipment, supplies	14	46	40
Service businesses	7	27	66
Services, other	9	30	61
Wearing apparel, wholesale	—	54	46
All others	11	22	67

B. METHODS OF COMPENSATION

	1955	1959	1964	1968
Salary plans	36%	40%	37%	27%
Straight salary	14	18	15	11
Salary & bonus	22	22	22	16
Commission plans	27	23	25	26
Straight commission	17	14	13	15
Commission with draw	10	9	12	11
Combination plans	37	37	38	47
Salary, bonus & commission	8	10	6	13
Salary & commission	29	27	32	34

"Compensation Methods by Industry" and "Methods of Compensation" are reprinted from *Compensation of Salesmen* with permission of the publisher, The Dartnell Corporation.

monthly. The deferred profit-sharing type of arrangement by which a salesman receives a notice telling him that money is being put away for him—while a builder of security in his mind—will not obtain the greatest possible effort to close more sales.

Salesmen's expense accounts are a perennial problem in many companies. Per diem rates for travel can be established and save companies argument and bookkeeping expenses, but the question of how much can and should be spent for entertainment of customers is a difficult one. Some companies make an arbitrary decision as to how much each salesman may spend in this regard each month, with the sales manager's specific approval required if a salesman is to go over that amount and be reimbursed. Others "play it by ear" and roughly add up the salesman's total compensation and his expense account, viewing the resulting total in the light of the sales he is producing.

To sum up the question of planning for and controlling direct selling costs, it is evident that accounting techniques, while not the ultimate answer, can be extremely helpful in assuring management that it is getting good value for each dollar spent.

Advertising and Promotion

Advertising and promotion have long been viewed as defying a rational approach, let alone the use of accounting techniques. In actuality, three major questions arise in this area: (1) What are you trying to do? (2) How much will you spend? (3) How should expenditures be allocated? We have looked at this problem earlier in this book, but here let us note that the advertising objectives of a company can usually be stated in accounting terms. Whether the aim is a specific dollar volume at certain product prices, a definite percentage of the total market, or a stated return on investment, each of these aims can and should be stated in quantitative (accounting) terms. If your aims are stated in dollars and cents or in percentages, you are much more likely to take a logical planned approach to your advertising program.

For years many companies have determined the amount to be spent on advertising as a percentage of anticipated or past sales. The fallaciousness of this reasoning should be apparent. If you anticipate a bad year, you spend less money on advertising; if you look forward to a good year, you spend much more. It would be interesting to see what would happen to companies bold enough to fly in the face of tradition, who looking forward to a bad year, increase their advertising. It is likely they would increase their share of the market and produce over-all profits substantially better than those of the industry in general.

If you concede that the percentage of anticipated sales is not a good basis for establishing an advertising budget, what alternatives are there? Planning an advertising budget should be the same type of process as planning for anything else. The amount to be spent must be determined by what you are trying to do, what your competitors are doing, and what your financial limitations are.

In passing, one old bit of psychology is worth noting. It is usually easier to get management to approve a major advertising campaign for a new product than to get an increased appropriation for an established product. New products may be planned to go from eighteen to forty-two months before breaking into the black, primarily because of heavy advertising expenditures, with no complaints by management. But woe to the individual who suggests that profit be cut even 1 per cent to protect an already successful product.

Industry norms are most interesting, but there appears to be no rationale for wide swings in the amount of advertising expenditures among industries. Table 6–3 shows advertising as a per cent of sales.

Advertising expenditures have held amazingly stable as a percentage of sales over the last few years, not varying more than a few hundredths of a percentage point from 1.18 per cent over-all. In interpreting this table, note that consumer advertising and industrial advertising have been lumped together. For example, within the broad classification "Chemicals" the average expenditures for

TABLE 6–3

ADVERTISING AS A PER CENT OF SALES

Manufacturing

Chemicals	4.26
Perfume, cosmetics, toilet preparations	13.09
Soap, related products	11.22
Drugs	9.42
Beer, related products	6.90
Soft drinks	6.17
Tobacco	5.81
Watches, clocks	5.21
Toys, sporting goods	4.26
Book publishing	3.57
Household appliances	2.81
Tires, inner tubes	2.29
Household furniture	1.12
Motor vehicles	1.11
Paper, allied products	0.84
Textile mill products	0.56
Primary metals	0.34

Wholesale, Retail Trade

Mail order houses	6.78
Jewelry	3.45
Department stores	2.91
Furniture, home furnishings	2.87
Food stores	1.27
Miscellaneous wholesale trade	0.57

"Advertising as a Per Cent of Sales." Reprinted with permission, *Advertising Age*, No. 4, 1968. Copyright, 1968, Advertising Publications, Inc.

advertising are 4.26 per cent of the sales dollar. However, certain subcategories within "Chemicals" showed higher percentages. Perfumes and cosmetics reported advertising as 13.09 per cent of the sales dollar; soaps and detergents reported 11.22 per cent; drugs reported 9.42 per cent. Traditionally, industrial advertising (one business advertising to other businesses) has been a relatively small percentage of the sales dollar, as witness the "Primary metals" figures in the table.

Companies pushing brand-name consumer products are most likely to spend a larger part of their sales dollars in advertising.

Further, companies with the widest gross profit margin should have more money available for advertising. It is not unusual for proprietary drug and cosmetic manufacturers to spend 20 to 40 per cent of their sales dollars to advertise a given product and still show a handsome profit.

The wide range of advertising expenditures among industries, when expressed as a percentage of either sales or gross profits, however, tends to indicate that there is no absolute by which to measure expenditures. Most people, for example, tend to think of motor vehicle manufacturers as major advertisers. They are, in total dollars spent, but they are among the lowest spenders in terms of expenditures as a percentage of sales (Table 6–3).

Every industry budgets its advertising differently. A company is almost forced to keep up with its competition. How far beyond competition it should go will depend upon what it is trying to accomplish, how much this accomplishment is likely to cost, and how much it can afford to spend.

Physical Distribution Expenses

Most managers readily agree that physical distribution costs break down into transportation expenses and costs of warehousing and handling. But few seem to realize that the cost of maintaining finished-goods inventory levels is also a physical distribution cost, and that all three of these factors are closely interrelated.

All too often a rate clerk will determine the route to be used in shipping a finished product by choosing the cheapest rate that will get the product delivered when needed. If the total of physical distribution costs is thought of as an entity, many companies might find that they need no warehouses, that their level of finished-goods inventory can be cut substantially, and that they save a great deal of handling and storage costs by shipping all orders by air directly from a central point. The previously mentioned rate clerk might well save the company shipping costs by shipping in carload lots by train to warehouses and having orders filled from the warehouses. On the other hand, if the warehouse were not in existence, the seemingly high-priced air freight might total far less than the combined cost of rail shipment and warehouse maintenance, let alone the possibility that inventory levels necessary to provide desired delivery schedules might well be cut sharply.

Physical distribution costs should be considered as an entity, not as three separate areas (transportation, warehousing, and inventory levels), each operating autonomously. Perhaps a specific example of the interaction of these areas will help establish the point.

Let us assume that a manufacturer of consumer and replacement electronic parts, the ABC Electronic Components Company, distributes through wholesalers. The product line has national distribution and customers are serviced from twenty-four company-leased warehouses in various parts of the country. The company has an enviable record for service and prides itself on its record of 95 per cent deliveries within twenty-four hours of receipt of order. It manufactures at just one location, where the master stock of finished goods is maintained. Production is based upon master-stock levels, where minimum-maximum levels to ensure service are maintained.

The ABC Company had sales of $20 million last year, and net income (after taxes) of $1 million. Master-stock inventory of finished goods averages $3 million, and stocks carried in the warehouses average $4 million.

Each warehouse orders merchandise weekly, with interim special orders as customers demand. Warehouse inventory levels are set based on lead times of two to twelve days' transportation time from master stock.

At this point, a new marketing director asks about the economics of air shipments directly to the customer and the elimination of warehouses versus the continuation of present methods. The comparative figures are shown in Table 6–4.

Looking at these figures, it would appear that the present method of warehouse operation is somewhat less expensive ($140,000) than the elimination of warehouses via use of air freight. This same

TABLE 6–4

Cost of Physical Distribution	Shipments to Warehouse	Shipments to Customer
Transportation:		
Surface	$ 600,000	$ 100,000
Air freight		1,150,000
Local delivery	150,000	70,000
Warehousing:		
Rent	210,000	10,000
Salaries	260,000	80,000
Insurance	70,000	40,000
Taxes	30,000	20,000
Other	60,000	20,000
Communications	90,000	120,000
Total yearly distribution costs	$1,470,000	$1,610,000

study, however, revealed that the desired delivery and customer service could be maintained with an average of $4 million inventory in central stock. The elimination of warehouse inventories would thus reduce total average finished-goods inventories by $3 million.

The pertinent question now is what does it cost the ABC Company to carry $3 million of excess inventory? The value or cost of money to the going business concern is a much-debated question. The exact cost is undeterminable, as mentioned in Chapter 10, but this cost has been estimated at 22 to 32 per cent per annum of the inventory values. Although the precise figures are unobtainable, we can rely on several rules of thumb that have gained acceptance. Table 6–5 should be prefaced with the reminder that we are here

TABLE 6–5

COSTS OF EXCESS INVENTORIES

Cost of capital	10%
Excess handling	2
Obsolescence	7
Deterioration	2
Controls	1
Total costs	22%

considering the potential costs that a going business must take into account when it undertakes to convert capital to a profit.

In addition to these costs, many analysts would insist on another factor, commonly referred to as profit risk, which might be as high as 10 per cent. Risk in this sense goes beyond the technical obsolescence or the physical deterioration of inventories and encompasses less predictable areas, such as price changes, variable market conditions, and planning failures. In essence the 10 per cent risk factor, when considered as an element of cost, is what allows a management that is right only nine out of ten times to make a profit.

If, however, the new marketing director remains conservative and puts aside the 10 per cent risk factor, elimination of warehouse inventories will result in annual savings of 22 per cent of $3 million, or $660,000.

Although this example may be somewhat overdrawn the fact is that an examination of physical distribution costs as an entity can pay major dividends. No longer should the traffic clerk merely consult rate tables to determine how goods should be shipped.

The foregoing example has deliberately overlooked possible savings in manufacturing costs brought about by manufacturing for one inventory as opposed to twenty-five. Moreover, this example is in no way an attempt to promote air freight.

In effect, detailed planning of an operation as a whole may produce better over-all results than planning each segment of an operation on its own. The best decisions for each department, considered on its own, do not necessarily produce a sum total of the best decisions for the company as a whole.

Summary

The value of budget preparation in the marketing area, is that management is forced to think and plan ahead. Budget preparation makes essential the reconsideration of why things are being done the same way they have been for years. The continuous "cut-and-fit" procedure that goes on in budget preparation is particularly obvious in the marketing area. The final budget, however, gives top management a tool for control, for when actual results vary from the budget they are subject to immediate examination. Budgeting is a time-consuming job, but top management should spend more time in review and appraisal of budgets than in any other activity. This is real planning, and it pays off.

Closely tied to the marketing field, and varying with some of the decisions made in creating the marketing budget, are the other functions of the business: production, research and development, finance and accounting, and administration. None of these operations can stand still while changing decisions are being made in the marketing area.

7   Producing the Goods

No manufacturing man likes to admit it, but the production department is at the mercy of the sales department. In a well-planned operation, sales department needs are expressed well ahead of time, which gives the production department time to plan so that goods can be produced in the most economical manner. In many companies, however, where advanced planning is not done, the manufacturing area must concentrate on getting the goods out at almost any cost.

From the manufacturing viewpoint, there are obvious advantages in knowing well ahead of time even an approximation of what finished products are expected and when. The unit cost of making limited numbers of a part, for example, may be twenty or even fifty times as much as the unit cost of making that part in larger quantities. Balancing the cost of carrying large inventories in numbers against producing those parts which can be immediately used is one of the production man's major decisions.

Basically the two extremes in production operations among companies are the so-called "process" industries and the "job shop." Process industries, which include such operations as refining oil, milling grain, and making paper, normally are highly automated and require relatively few people to carry on the operation. At the other end of the spectrum, the job shop produces items to order. In the job shop handcrafting is usually part of the operation, and a much higher percentage of total costs is skilled labor. Since the great bulk of America's manufacturing operations are somewhere in between these two extremes, it is virtually impossible to postulate a single method of planning and control that will be best for all.

Elements of Production

Any company faces three possible limitations to its production: supplies of raw material, supplies of labor, and plant capacity. In planning for maximum production efficiency, each of these factors must be considered. When any one of these factors appears to limit production of the goods desired, various short-term remedies may be taken. If the same factor consistently inhibits production, long-term planning to overcome the deficiency is the answer.

Some of the short-term expediencies which may be necessary, and in some cases desirable even if one is not confronted with the problem, are these: simplifying the work involved in manufacturing a product, extending plant operations to two or even three shifts per day, using alternative raw materials, working overtime, establishing incentive pay, improving plant layout, redesigning the product to remove bottlenecks in production, subcontracting of work to the outside, renting or purchasing additional buildings and machinery, and better organizing the work flow through the factory. Enumerating these possible solutions of the problem serves to point out that if the top production man knows what is expected of him for a period of time ahead, he will not have to resort to costly last-minute improvisations, but will be able to make long-range plans which allow the products to be made most economically.

For the purpose of this chapter, we shall assume that the top production man has at least some advance notice as to what is to be expected of him, and that his problems are then limited to producing the amount of product desired, by the desired time, of consistently high quality, at minimum cost.

Since the cost elements of a manufacturing operation are materials, direct labor, and overhead, we shall discuss each briefly.

Materials

Depending upon the type and extent of the manufacturing operation, the term "materials" may refer to raw materials, semifabricated materials, parts, subassemblies, assemblies, or in some cases the total product. For the purpose of this section, materials are anything purchased from outside. In planning and control of materials, two major considerations are: the actual buying and receipt of materials, and controlling them once you have them.

The buying function typically is handled by a purchasing department, which may consist of the part-time services of one person or, in larger corporations, the full time of hundreds of people. In buying materials, three factors must be considered. One of these, of course, is quality. The buyer must know what quality standards are necessary and must be sure that the supplier understands these. Second, reliability of delivery is important. Failure to get materials of even a minor nature to the production line may cause a work stoppage, which is most expensive. Other considerations are the quantity and the price of the materials to be bought.

In well-planned production, the production schedule that details all the goods to be produced for a given time ahead is analyzed. Then, for each of the products to be produced, a "bill of materials" is prepared which is merely a detailed breakdown of all of the items to be used—with the quantities of each—in producing the product. Once a bill of materials is prepared, it is checked against inventory on hand, and the decision is made as to which items should be ordered. It is at this point in the planning that major amounts of money can be saved or wasted.

It would seem simple to order only those items which do not appear in inventory and in the quantities necessary for immediate use in production. Several other factors, however, must now be considered, for example: What sort of quantity discounts are available, if relatively large quantities of individual items are ordered? What are the differences in shipping costs if a carload lot can be ordered instead of a less-than-carload lot? What are the chances of spoilage in the manufacturing operations, which might lead to demands for more raw materials than the original bill of materials showed? All these considerations and others must be weighed against the cost of carrying inventories in excess of minimum needs. On the other side of the picture is the possibility of obsolescence. Suppose changes in the product line take place, with the result that certain parts or materials are no longer needed?

This brings us to the second part of the materials function: the control of inventory. Although the physical control of inventory—the safekeeping function—is important, the term "inventory control" implies a much broader function. As indicated in Chapter 2, the cost of materials used over a given period can be found by adding the materials on hand at the beginning of the period to the purchases made during the period and subtracting the materials on hand at the end of the period. Although many smaller businesses still arrive at their earnings statement in this manner, it is obviously a major chore to have to count all your inventories every time you want profit and loss information. As a result, most companies now keep perpetual inventory records, which show quantities of each item of inventory on hand at all times. These records start with the balance on hand at the beginning of the period; all goods received are added to this balance, and all withdrawals from stock are deducted. Normally, a physical inventory—an actual count of the items on hand—is made once a year, and the perpetual inventory records are adjusted to reflect this actual count. Any well-designed and controlled system for handling inventories will result in only minor adjustments to the records as a result of this count.

If quantities of items on hand were the only concern, the operation of an inventory control system would be much simpler than it actually is. Besides quantities, however, we must keep track of what has been paid for the various items of inventory. Since even relatively small manufacturing enterprises may have as many as two or three thousand different items in stock, and prices for an individual item may vary markedly in any one accounting period, it can readily be seen that keeping inventory records in detail can be a major, costly chore. Depending on the company's situation, there are a number of alternatives to reduce this record-keeping function. A time-honored rule of thumb states that in most companies 85 per cent of the cost of items in inventory may be accounted for by some 15 per cent of the items. If this is true in any given situation, one answer to the problem of costly inventory controls is to concentrate on the 15 per cent of the items which make up the biggest share of the dollar costs. For the 85 per cent of the items which account for relatively little of the total cost, short cuts can be used. The resultant savings may overcome any objections to some inaccuracy and reduced controls.

In planning for a manufacturing operation and in forecasting actual product costs, materials are often a very important element of total costs. In preparing a manufacturing budget, prices paid for materials must be assumed, as well as the quantities of materials to be used. Thus, any variations from the budget or manufacturing plan having to do with materials are either price variances (paying different amounts for the materials than anticipated), or quantity variances (using different amounts of material than expected).

Pricing materials issued to production, so that the cost of these materials will be included in the final product cost, is difficult, as we have seen. In a sense, the ideal way of handling this would be to charge to production the actual cost of the materials issued. In many cases, however, this is impractical, because similar materials are stored together and become so intermingled that it is difficult to establish the identity of any particular shipment's origin or price.

The subject of standard costs will be discussed in more detail later in this chapter, but some mention of its application to materials cost should be made here. Under a standard-cost system for materials, the manufacturing budget assumes that certain specific costs will be paid for each item of material. As goods are received, any variation in price paid from the "standard cost" is in effect set aside as a price variance, and the manufacturing cost of the product being made is charged only with the standard cost of the materials being purchased. This price variance account, then, can be analyzed from time to time to see where prices are going off the track, and action can be taken to correct the situation immediately. If standard costs are not used, the effect of price changes tends to be buried in the over-all cost of the product manufactured, and a major job of analysis may be necessary to determine why costs of the product have fluctuated.

In brief, the problem of planning and controlling materials encompasses obtaining the materials, handling the materials within the plant, and allocating the cost of these materials to the various products being made. A good planning and control system for materials will result in reduction of risk of loss from misappropriation or theft, control of loss through obsolescence, control of amounts of money tied up in inventory, and up-to-the-minute information for management on an exception basis, showing where things are going differently from the plan, so that remedial action may be taken.

Direct Labor

The wages of employees working directly on a product are known as "direct labor costs." By and large, direct labor is paid in one of two ways: by "piecework," in which the employee is paid so much per piece produced, or by "day work," in which the employee is paid a stated hourly rate regardless of the function to which he is assigned. Planning and control of direct labor has two aims: to obtain the maximum amount of work from each of the employees, and to make certain that product costs reflect proper labor charges.

Over the years more attention has been paid to planning and control of direct labor operations than any other phase of business. For this reason, along with the essential simplicity of direct labor operations, most businesses are fairly well run in this area. In the first place, direct labor operations are normally of a type for which engineered standards can be set. Even if an operator performs a dozen different operations in a day, these operations are usually done often enough to make it worthwhile to determine what the standards on the operation should be. Our use of the word "standard" implies the amount of time it should take an average operator to perform a function. In the second place, since almost all direct labor can be identified with a specific product, there is relatively little difficulty in determining where direct labor costs should be charged.

Thus, in planning a production budget the production manager knows how many units are to be produced and what operations go into the production of these units; he can plan then how many man-hours will be necessary and at what job classifications and rates of pay. The control function is equally clear cut. When actual results are reported, they are compared with the plan and quickly reveal where, if at all, plans went astray.

The concept of "standard hours" is often valuable in production planning and budgeting. A standard hour represents the amount of work a man should do in an hour. If the budget for a particular product is expressed in standard hours of labor and a labor rate increase is put into effect, computation of the new cost is relatively simple. Hence many companies maintain standard hours for the jobs involved in each of their products.

Briefly, standards can be set several ways. The decision involving what method to use in setting standards is an economic one. The more detailed, and hence more accurate, standard is more costly to set. For this reason only truly repetitive jobs call for really engineered standards. Relatively infrequent jobs may be measured by such means as average actual over the years, random sampling, or a limited-cycle time-study operation. A description of these various methods of measurement is found in Chapter 9.

In summary, once direct labor standards are set, their incorporation and use in planning and control is relatively simple.

Overhead

Overhead, or "burden," is the name for all those costs which cannot be specifically identified with any one product. These include such items as supervision, maintenance, fuel, rent, depreciation, purchasing, production planning, and record keeping in general.

Planning and control of overhead items has two major aims: to minimize costs wherever they occur, and to ensure that overhead is allocated in the best possible manner to the various products being manufactured. At the outset, let us distinguish between variable and fixed overhead charges. For example, electric power used to run productive machines is variable, in that it tends to rise with the amount of activity of the machine involved, which is directly related to the products produced. On the other hand, depreciation on a factory remains the same regardless of the amount of productivity at any given time. Of course, much of the overhead of any operation is neither completely fixed nor completely variable. Depreciation on a machine, for example, would be regarded as a fixed cost. On the other hand, if production is desired in quantities greater than one machine can produce, another machine might be purchased. Depreciation on that second machine would be an additional item of overhead costs. Hence, many items of overhead might well be termed semivariable.

Probably the best method of planning for overhead expenses and controlling them is by grouping them in "cost centers." A cost center is in effect a department of the factory. Each of these departments must be under the jurisdiction of one administrative authority. This is an application of "responsibility accounting," as mentioned in Chapter 3. Cost centers are of two different kinds: production departments and service departments.

For example, all machine tools of about the same size that are automatically controlled, at least in some degree, might well be grouped in one production cost center under the direction of one foreman. Indirect costs of that particular area should then be gathered and made the responsibility of that foreman. Such items as setup time, maintenance, depreciation, and supervision in connection with this department would make up the overhead statement for the department. Once this plan is set up, the foreman should be told that he has responsibility for controlling these costs within certain limits.

An example of a service department cost center might be the storerooms. The head storekeeper would be held accountable for the numbers of people and the rates of pay in his department, for stationery and supplies, and for all other costs directly chargeable to his operation.

There are some overhead items which no one, except possibly the plant manager, controls. These, too, should be grouped together; they would include such items as rent or depreciation on the building as a whole, administrative salaries, etc.

The essentials of a plan for preparing a manufacturing budget, and hence the tools necessary to control overhead costs, are now fairly clear. The question then is: How should these various overhead cost centers be charged to the different products being made? There is no one answer to this problem, though common sense will generally dictate the best course of action. In a process cost operation, for example, overhead of a given cost center is frequently apportioned to different products that have been processed on the basis of the common function or operation performed. In this case the unit selected will be the most convenient one by which to measure the operation. Thus in one department, the unit may be the number of linear feet of lumber sawed; in another, the number of board feet planed; while in others the number of units of each product produced might be the basis for apportioning overhead. In the job cost system, the cost unit, of course, is always the function of the producing departments.

Distribution of service department cost-center costs is even less susceptible to rules. Purchasing department costs, for example, might well be apportioned on the basis of the number of purchase orders written for each product. On the other hand, in this same department total dollar volume of purchases might be a fairer measure of the activity of the department on which to base the apportionment of its cost.

A major trap into which many companies have fallen in some measure, in the overhead area, is the concentration upon gathering and allocating costs rather than upon controlling them. It should be emphasized, however, that to set up a system for actually controlling overhead costs in a factory, it may be necessary to make major changes in the organizational structure of the factory.

Standard Costs

To those who are primarily concerned with the preparation or analysis of financial statements, the term "standard cost" brings to mind an accounting system in which inventories are valued at a predetermined or standard cost, with any differences or variances between the standard cost and actual costs being set aside, out of inventories, and usually charged to operations as incurred. An illustration of this thought pattern would look something like Figure 7–1 (page 76).

If asked to justify the expense involved in developing standards, the accountant might answer that the separation of variances makes it possible to maintain inventory records without a continual re-evaluation of them based on constantly changing actual costs. In many cases he is right. The savings obtainable, through eliminating the cost accounting task of establishing new unit costs every time an acceptable framework from a financial statement–inventory cost records, frequently outweigh the cost of developing the standards.

His main concern is developing the standards as inexpensively as possible, and changing them as infrequently as possible, within an acceptable framework from a financial statement–inventory valuation standpoint.

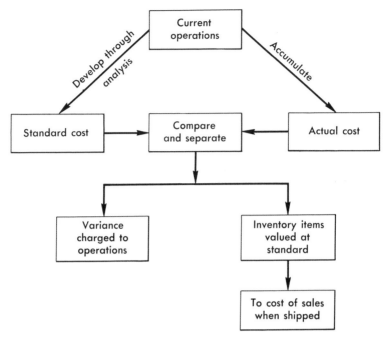

Figure 7–1. The Accountant's View of a Standard Cost System

From a management control viewpoint, a standard cost plan means something quite different. The above-mentioned savings in accounting effort are only a minor concern. The main concern should be controlling costs: finding variances from the standard promptly, and finding out who, or what organization, or what type of failure caused the variance, and correcting it. The psychological impact of reports identifying the organizations responsible for variances, and the accompanying management emphasis stressing performance at standard, causes operating people to preplan their activities and in general to become more cost-conscious. The most useful picture of a standard cost plan looks something like Figure 7–2.

Certainly from the standpoint of obtaining maximum profits, the management control concept of standard costs is more impor-

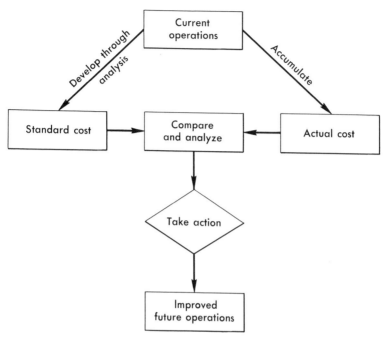

Figure 7–2. The Manager's View of a Standard Cost System

tant than the "eliminate detail accounting" point of view. Without some form of control system it is often impossible to motivate total effort consistently toward the objective of maximum profits. As we go further down the line in organizational patterns, people tend to lose the entrepreneurial incentive. The profit and loss statement is too far removed from the first-line supervisor for him to be consistently concerned with it as a form of performance index. The standard-cost plan of the "management control" variety provides the supervisor with a personalized measuring stick—gives him a goal to strive for and a basis for recognition if he achieves it. Companies using this technique successfully are generally rewarded far in excess of any investment made in the system.

Use of standards as a control device, however, imposes some severe restrictions on how standards are set. Competition arises among supervisors on their performance against standard; thus, inconsistencies between standards in their difficulty of achievement competely invalidate the competitive urge. To be effective, therefore, standards must be set consistently, one against the other.

Further, a concept of "reasonable expectancy" must be applied in setting standards so that management can deal in absolute control. For instance, if standards based on some ideal concept of performance were set, it would not be possible to know with certainty just what level of performance compared to standard should be considered acceptable. If, on the other hand, standards were set on a basis of reasonable expectancy (that is, what should be expected, based on normal effort and skills and present conditions), efforts could be directed positively toward a goal of 100 per cent performance. The drawback to this approach appears when we realize that standards set under the "reasonable expectancy" approach must be adjusted each time changes in shop methods are put into effect. This situation, while not a major problem, does cause some difficulties in that changes in standards make it necessary to adjust inventory values. Such changes also destroy the historical significance of variance figures, since the base for arriving at the variance shifts so frequently that problems arise in valuing inventories in accordance with accepted accounting principles.

Another complication is that, without knowing all the problems involved, top management often wants to know actual costs by part and by product line on a unit-cost basis. They argue that costs should be available as a basis for setting prices for products and adjusting prices if cost patterns so indicate (competition permitting). After long explanations on the cumbersome nature of accounting for costs by part and on how standards can be used in pricing (estimated standard on new products factored by past variance experience), they frequently accept the standard-cost plan—on one condition, "Variance data must be accumulated for each product line." This makes little sense. If standards are set consistently, variance performance is a condition of time or of failure in duties, not attributable to a specific product but to a specific organization. Splitting variance by product classes is artificial and expensive from a record-keeping point of view in any area of operations where more than one product class is manufactured, and such artificial splitting detracts from the clear-cut identity of organizational responsibility for variances.

Case Study

A case study may be helpful in examining the values of standard costs.

A company manufactures one product: Y, a plastic article made in a single process from Z raw material. The cycle time to manufacture Y is less than one day.

The company has an actual process-type cost system accounting separately for:

1. Direct labor—charged to labor costs based on payrolls
2. Material—requisitioned to work-in-process based on actual cost of Z purchased
3. Overhead—allocated based on labor hours

Production records are maintained so that we know how many finished units of Y are made daily.

The cost system involves:

1. Accumulating direct shop labor, material and overhead costs incurred by months, and dividing by the number of units of Y completed, to arrive at a unit cost of so many finished items
2. Keeping records of how many items of Y are on hand at certain prices, so that when we sell we can reduce our inventory at the actual cost of the items sold

Now let us see what this system does for us. Assume the unit-cost accumulation data appear as in Table 7–1.

Ys are being sold at $4.00, and are producing a comfortable margin of profit. However, the owner of the business has some disturbing news: He claims that the market could be increased 300 per cent if Ys could be sold for $3.00. He says that a competitor

TABLE 7–1

Unit Cost Per Y Manufactured

	Month 1	Month 2	Month 3	Month 4	Weighted Average
Direct labor	$1.08	$1.12	$1.90	$ .60	$1.19
Overhead	1.12	1.37	2.01	.72	1.32
Material	.84	.81	.87	1.00	.85
Total	$3.04	$3.30	$4.78	$2.32	$3.36

plans to sell an identical item for $3.25. He declares that $3.00 is a reasonable price, since we made the item for $2.32 in Month 4.

The accountant disagrees, and the shop man supports him. Our average cost has been in the $3.25 to $3.50 range for six months. How can we sell the item for $3.00? The shop man says there was an error in counting finished units between Month 3 and Month 4 and the figures seem to support him. The owner raises the question whether anyone has any idea what the item really should cost, and there is general agreement that the best indication we have is based on past performance.

Now let us see what the figures would show if a standard cost were developed for Product Y. The following steps were taken:

1. An analysis of purchasing records reveals that raw material Z should cost about 40 cents per pound based on market conditions in the foreseeable future. The head of purchasing agrees.

2. An engineering analysis of Product Y indicates that each unit requires just under 2 pounds of Z raw material. Based on evaluation of unavoidable waste, the shop manager agrees that he can make Ys at an average of 2 pounds of Z per unit.

3. Discussion with the accountant indicates that $2 per hour is a reasonable average labor rate for direct-labor workers, providing that we don't have highly skilled workers doing lower-paid jobs. The shop manager agrees.

4. A time study of three or four fairly representative workers indicates that a normally skilled worker with plenty to do should make one Y in 20 minutes, or .334 hour. The shop manager dis-

agrees at first but after going over the time studies admits the standard seems fair.

5. All the managers get together and agree on departmental overhead budgets at a level of production which seems reasonable for the next year. When the budgets are related to projected labor for the same period, the overhead amounts to 100 per cent of projected direct labor.

The facts established to arrive at a standard cost per unit of Y are shown in Table 7–2.

TABLE 7–2

Element	Basis	Per Unit of Y
Direct labor	.334 hr. @ $2.00	$ .67
Overhead	100% of direct labor	.67
Material	2 lbs. of Z @ $.40	.80
Total		$2.14

The result may well surprise everyone concerned. Yet all have participated in developing the standard in one way or another and would like to see it work. Now the problem is to produce the product at this standard cost. Here are the steps taken:

1. The accounts payable group is to charge anything over or under 40 cents per pound paid for Z raw material to a special variance account. There are to be weekly meetings where the head of purchasing is to explain any such variances.

2. In making up the payroll journal, hours are to be charged to work-in-process at $2. Anything over or under the $2 average rate is to be charged to a separate variance account, and the accountant and the shop manager are to explain these variances at weekly meetings.

3. The storeroom is to issue only 2 pounds of Z for each Y scheduled for completion. Production is to be continued until the scheduled quantity is reached. If more Z is required, the storeroom will report the excess usage to accounting who will charge its cost

to a separate variance account. A separate flash report will be discussed with the shop manager daily.

4. Each day, the output of Ys will be multiplied by the .334 standard-hour figure. The difference between this figure and the number of actual hours worked by shop people represents efficiency loss or gain. This efficiency figure will be provided to the shop man daily. The efficiency gain or loss is to be extended at the $2 standard rate plus the 100 per cent applied overhead and charged to a separate variance account.

5. The departmental overhead budgets agreed to as the basis for the 100 per cent overhead rate are to be used to determine just what departments were over or under their overhead budgets by months. A special report is to be prepared for top-management discussion, and any amounts over or under budgets are to be charged to a separate variance account.

Table 7–3 shows the results obtained through the standard-cost plan and some remarks on how these results were brought about.

TABLE 7–3

	Month 5	Month 6	Month 7	Month 8	Month 9
Variance analysis					
Material price	$ 1,800	$ 0	$ 300	$ 0	$ 0
Labor rate	200	100	(100)	300	100
Material usage	18,000	12,000	3,000	1,000	500
Labor efficiency	7,000	4,000	1,000	700	100
Overhead rate	0	4,000	0	100	(200)
	$27,000	$20,100	$4,200	$2,100	$ 500
No. of units produced	50,000	50,000	50,000	50,000	50,000
Variance per unit	$ .54	$ .40	$ .08	$ .04	$ .01
Standard unit cost	2.14	2.14	2.14	2.14	2.14
Actual cost	$2.68	$2.54	$2.22	$2.18	$2.15

The variance picture at the end of Month 5 looked somewhat dismal. True, costs were down below the previous average, but everyone was concerned about the variances due to material price and usage and labor efficiency.

Cash, from day to day
Backlog of sales orders
Materials on hand and on order
Production
Sales

Accordingly, he is pretty well on top of the situation and has most facts at hand on which to base reasoned judgments.

As his business expands, however, he must depend on others to observe, measure, and record, and to communicate these measurements to him, either verbally or in writing. It is at this point that MIS comes into the picture.

Every business and every function of a business needs MIS. Four main problem areas of a typical business are the following:

1. *Marketing* (the prime source of revenues in most cases)
   a. How did we do?
      What were our sales by product, customer, and salesman and how did they compare to our planned sales?
      What were our sales as a share of the market, compared to our competition?
   b. What should we expect?
      What is the backlog of sales orders?
      What are the trends of the population and its buying habits?
2. *Production*
   a. How did we do?
      What were the costs per product compared to what we expected?
   b. What should we expect?
      Are costs going up or down, and why?
3. *Finance*
   a. Where do we stand?
      How are we doing on collection of receivables?
      Can we pay our bills? What is the cash on hand?
   b. What do we expect?
      How much money will we need in the future and where will we get it?
      What are the trends in the money market which might guide us to best solutions?
4. *Research and Development*
   a. How did we do?

What concrete accomplishments have been made? Why and at what costs?
b. Where should future efforts be pointed?
How should we invest future monies to produce the best results?

This outline of some of the major problems of a business indicates some areas of management decision making in which MIS can help. Obviously, in many of these areas Operations Research can be helpful in guiding decision making, but only if the facts on what has happened and is likely to happen (MIS) are available.

Of course, the art of communication enters into any MIS. The information being transmitted must be understood as easily and quickly as possible. Earlier, we envisioned the busy executive up to his hips in paper. Can you imagine trying to read the *New York Times* or the *Wall Street Journal* without titles, subheadings, or summaries of important articles? The fact that "it's all there" is hardly a comfort to the busy executive.

The breadth and level of detail of information given to the manager must be limited, and he should receive information only about those activities for which he is responsible. For example, the salesman does not need current production information, but he does need data on deliveries of the product he is selling. The president does not need details of what is happening on the production line. He does need enough information to monitor major problems in production.

Also, all executives need an information system which will flag all major items that are not going according to plan (see Management by Exception in Chapter 3).

In the future, well-constructed Management Information Systems will become increasingly important for the following reasons:

1. The complexity and magnitude of business operations will continue to grow.

2. The ability of management to use more information (more intelligent managers) will increase.

3. There will be growing use of specialists for specific problems

to be solved by Operations Research and other quantitative methods, and better facts must be available for them.

4. The ability to store and manipulate information will continue its rapid growth. For example, in the last decade, costs per computation have decreased by 100 to 1; costs of storage have decreased 1,000 to 1; and speed has increased 1,000 to 1. We can look forward to the time when all pertinent facts about a business will be stored in a computer, ready to pop out as asked for, and at a reasonable price.

5. Long-distance transmission of information is rapidly becoming faster and cheaper.

6. The ability to communicate is improving very fast, in that facts can be presented in increasingly more relevant formats.

One final word—do not construct an MIS based upon asking the manager what he wants. He has been tied down too long by restraints on availability of information. Instead, tell him what he can have.

Summary

It might seem that the greater the amount of factual information available, the wiser management decisions become. Unfortunately this is not true, and many a manager is so bogged down in a morass of computer runs that he cannot distinguish important facts from insignificant ones.

A well-constructed MIS system is based upon the knowledge of what information is available, the cost of accumulating, storing and retrieving such information, and the relative importance of the various items of information in arriving at valid management decisions.

Each level of management has different information requirements. If operations are going according to plan, a minimum of information is needed on a day-to-day basis. When things are not going according to plan, a "red flag" should be raised as quickly as possible.

PART II

Management Uses of Accounting

Here is what the management group's discussion of variance indicated at the end of Month 5:

1. The purchasing agent stated he had gone over the 40 cents per pound standard for Z raw materials because of current price conditions, but that if he could hire two or three more purchasing people in the East close to where Z is obtained, and could spend additional money for travel and an Eastern office, he would guarantee meeting the 40 cents per pound standard. The management group decided to let him go ahead with this plan.

2. The shop manager was appalled at the material usage variance. He had been aware of the problem based on his daily flash reports and was working with engineering in designing some new die attachments which would eliminate the problem. It seemed that a high number of Ys were broken as they were taken out of the die. He had been aware of this in the past, but the problem had not been brought into focus from a cost standpoint until now.

3. On the subject of labor efficiency loss, the shop manager expressed the opinion that he was just now learning the value of shop-loading his employees. His daily flash reports told him of this loss early in the month, and he had been working with the industrial engineer to correct it. They had developed a plan where the standard was broken down so that each job in the process could be controlled. Each employee was given work sufficient for him or her to reach the standard, and causes of failure were being investigated. The investigation was revealing that some employees were not properly trained, others had been using improper tools, and some were just not producing. The shop manager guaranteed that they would conquer the problem and virtually eliminate the variance.

At the end of Month 6, definite progress had been made:

1. The material price variance was eliminated. The new purchasing people operating out of the Eastern office and traveling widely in their procurement efforts were obtaining Z at much lower prices.

2. Progress had been made using the new die to eliminate the

breakage problem and it looked as though we could forget about this problem in a month or two.

   3. Progress was evident in the labor efficiency variance area.

   4. An overhead rate variance developed as a result of the extra costs now generated by the purchasing department. But the accountant explained that he was getting rid of ten cost clerks who had been keeping track of unit costs of Y under the old system, and that the reduction in payroll cost would offset the unanticipated purchasing department expenses. (He no longer had to keep unit-cost records of Ys in inventory. They were valued at standard since all the variances had been charged against operations.)

At the end of Month 9, the results were obvious to all. Everyone had done his part as planned, and the company was evaluating the possibilities of expanding its market at the new, lower selling price.

Efforts to develop effective standard-cost controls generally fall into three classes:

   1. Education—gaining common understanding
   2. Implementation—installing the system
   3. Guided development—hand-feeding until it is actually working

It is important at the outset to develop a specific program covering all three of the phases. There appear to be strong advantages in establishing a committee of management people in all areas of production to be charged with the final responsibility for developing the plan.

Invariably, there is a certain resentment to change. It is of utmost importance that an undertaking of this magnitude have top-management support to alleviate any opposing pressures which may be so generated.

Incremental Costing

One of the major contributions to management thinking in recent years has been the development of incremental, or direct, costing methods. Incremental costing, as the name implies, puts all emphasis on what specific costs would be added or omitted if alternative decisions were to be made about what is or is not to be produced.

The bulk of this chapter has been concerned with the use of the more traditional absorption method of accounting, under which all costs in the manufacturing area end up being charged to some specific product or products. It should be recognized at this point that financial accounting requirements—reports to stockholders, to the SEC, and to banks—require absorption costing as a method of evaluating inventories. Financial accounting requirements, however, should not blind management to the facts that it needs for making policy decisions.

Incremental costing can be most useful in determining current pricing and output policy, evaluating proposals for cost reductions, making decisions on the purchase of minor capital items, deciding whether to make or buy parts of assemblies and whole assemblies, and determining whether to add or to drop a given product. All these decisions are generally a study of alternative choices. As such, they should be put in terms of balancing the added cost of a certain policy against the added revenue resulting from this policy. A company may not be able to use direct costing or incremental costing as the basis on which its books are kept, but it should use incremental costing frequently when a policy decision has to be made.

Only those costs which can be specifically identified with a given product are considered incremental costs. These costs include materials used, direct labor, and those items of overhead which can be directly attributed to the product. All fixed overhead costs (for example, rent, supervisory salaries, depreciation) are excluded. Incremental costing is useful only in making short-run decisions. In any long-term decision all costs, direct or indirect, must be absorbed by some product; it would be foolish, for example, to put up a new plant based on the production of a product that could be priced so that it returned only the direct costs involved.

Examples

Some examples of how data are used in the decision-making process may strengthen the argument for the use of incremental costing.

WHICH PRODUCT TO PUSH. In this example, a sales manager wanted to know on which product the sales force should put its major emphasis. The decision was to be based on how the company could make maximum profits. It had been determined that there was sufficient production flexibility to allow some shift in product output.

The accounting department prepared the calculation of per unit profit contributions shown in Table 7–4.

TABLE 7–4

	Product		
	A	*B*	*C*
Sales	$2.74	$3.21	$1.92
Cost of sales:			
Direct costs	$ .84	$1.16	$ .70
Overhead allocated	.45	.79	.39
Total cost of sales	$1.29	$1.95	$1.09
Gross profit	$1.45	$1.26	$ .83
Selling and administrative costs	.62	.56	.36
Income before taxes	$ .83	$ .70	$ .47

Using traditional accounting methods, the obvious decision would be to push Product A, because it returns a higher income before taxes than either of the other products.

A comparison of how the calculation would have looked under direct costing is shown in Table 7–5.

In this example of the same situation, the use of direct costs reveals that Product B contributes more than either A or C. The principle involved is that the overhead and administrative charges were going to be incurred in any event. Full costs based on absorp-

TABLE 7–5

	Product		
	A	*B*	*C*
Sales	$2.74	$3.21	$1.92
Direct costs:			
Manufacturing	$ .84	$1.16	$ .70
Sales	.21	.24	.18
Total direct costs	$1.05	$1.40	$ .88
Contribution to fixed costs and profits	$1.69	$1.81	$1.04

tion accounting and direct and relevant costs must be differentiated. A main factor in this decision and in many others is that the direct costs or incremental costs are those that bear on the problem and allocations can only confuse the issue.

MAKE OR BUY. In this example, a small manufacturing concern produced and sold a fairly complex product. The company was concerned primarily with the assembly of the product, for 85 per cent of its parts were purchased from outside. The company had, however, a small machine shop operation that manufactured parts. At the time of investigation, this machine operation was operating at about 50 per cent of capacity. An example of a make-or-buy calculation (to determine whether it would be more profitable for the company to make a given part or to buy it outside) is shown in Table 7–6.

These figures indicate that it is more desirable to purchase the part than to consider making it.

TABLE 7–6

Part Number 460	
Direct labor	$ .36
Direct material	.13
Overhead—at 360 per cent of direct labor	1.30
Total cost to make	$1.79
Cost to purchase	$1.37

Under direct costing the calculation would have been as shown in Table 7–7. This indicates clearly that since the capacity is available to make the part within the company's own facilities, it should be made there, and as a result the company will obtain a higher profit.

TABLE 7–7

Part Number 460

Direct labor	$ .36
Direct material	.13
Direct burden	.78
Total cost to make	$1.27
Cost to purchase	$1.37

Many conservative financial people, including many CPAs, argue that direct costing should not be used because direct-costing concepts cannot require absorption of full overhead. We will be the first to admit that these concepts should not be used in balance sheet presentations. In fact, if long-range decisions were made based upon direct costing, a company would soon direct-cost itself right out of business. We do contend, however, that on a separate study basis, direct costing can be an excellent tool for management whereby short-term plans can be made which will increase a company's profit.

Summary

Planning and control of manufacturing costs are considerably simplified if costs are first divided into three groups: materials, direct labor, and overhead. As a second step, management must push levels of responsibility down as low as possible. Each foreman should be held accountable for what he spends, whether it be in the material area, direct labor, or overhead. By decentralizing responsibility, including the lowest level of management in the budget-making process, and by making it clear to each participant that he must live within his budget, many of the desired goals can be met. Standard costs, while not a panacea, can be helpful in almost any situation in the planning and control of manufacturing costs. Incremental costing can and should be used in arriving at short-term decisions where alternative actions are possible.

8   Research and Development

There is probably no more difficult area to plan, evaluate, or control than that of research and development in modern business. Over $17 billion is being spent annually by United States corporations in research and development. In the past five to ten years, the amount being spent on research and development has increased between 8 and 10 per cent a year. When this is compared with an average increase of 5 per cent in the Gross National Product, it can readily be seen that this is an increasingly important area of business. Planning and controlling research and development expenses is such a problem to some people because they account for research and development as one area. But it is not one "ball of wax." It is composed of a number of different functions which have been grouped together in most companies merely for administrative convenience. If the various functions typically included in a research and development department are each considered separately, definitions such as these* might result:

Pure Research. A search for facts and knowledge without refer-

* G. W. Howard, *Common Sense in Research and Development* (Vantage Press, New York, 1955).

ence to their application. The motivation for this is scientific curiosity.

Fundamental Research. A search for new knowledge in a general field without reference to specific applications. The motivation is that any discovery can probably be applied by the organization doing the work.

Applied Research. A search for new knowledge directly related to a specific problem, and the application of all existing knowledge to practical solution of the problem.

Development. Extension of findings and theories into practical application for experimental or demonstration purposes, including the construction and testing of experimental models.

Following development, products normally go to production engineering, where the best way to make them is determined. For the purpose of this chapter, we have included the operation of the research and development department with the development of a prototype model of the product. Perhaps it would be helpful if we considered accounting for each of these functions separately.

Pure and Fundamental Research

The distinction between pure and fundamental research is clearly stated above. But from the standpoint of planning and control, these two areas have many similarities, and we shall treat them as one.

There are no clear financial guidelines by which either pure or fundamental research may be planned and controlled. One thing is certain: only large companies should do either to any major degree. Investments in pure and fundamental research should really not be considered as expenses from the management viewpoint, but should be compared with alternative uses of capital (see Chapter 10). The question of how much should be spent in these areas is a function of what a company can afford and what the competition does in these areas.

On the other side of the coin, it is interesting to note that the secret to winning the American Management Association business strategy game is investment in research. No matter how stupidly the games are played, the team that puts the most into research usually comes out a winner. This is neither coincidental nor phantasmagoric. We cannot tell you how much should be put into pure and fundamental research, but we can say that if intelligently directed, it should be all you can afford.

The difficulties in planning and controlling pure and fundamental research are the following:

1. This area is nonrepetitive. It is unlike production, where standards can be set, because different things are being done all the time.

2. The outcome cannot be predicted. For example, a search for a cancer cure resulted in the finding of an animal feed additive. The feed additive was turned into a profitable item, but it was a far cry from what was being sought.

3. The time involved in developing anything concrete from pure or fundamental research is unpredictable. It has been contended that there is a seven-year average cycle, and that any department conducting pure and fundamental research should be judged on the basis of seven-year periods. This rough rule of thumb, however, seems almost useless in planning and controlling a research operation.

4. Neither the credit nor the responsibility for any specific development can be clearly assigned to one individual or team. The final product is often the product of previously discovered intangible ideas to which new theories have been applied.

5. Closely allied to the preceding point is the delayed impact of the basic ideas developed. Some of the theories developed in the 1920s at Du Pont, for example, are only now being translated into products which are making a profit for the company. And of course, completely different people are working on them.

6. The value of the results obtained is not clear until years after, if ever.

These are genuine difficulties in planning and evaluating the pure and fundamental research areas, but let us also consider the possible values.

1. A better understanding of phenomena may be obtained. This, although difficult to put a price on, may lead to major discoveries at some later time.

2. This type of research may well bring about a supply of new ideas for applied research.

3. The public relations value of doing pure and fundamental research should not be underestimated. Steinmetz of General Electric Company was worth millions of dollars to them whether or not he had ever developed a product on which they made a profit. He made General Electric a leader in the field of research.

4. Pure and fundamental research, when carried on successfully, can give a company a great jump on its competition. If competition is investing heavily in pure and fundamental research, it is incumbent on all those who expect to be leaders in the field to do likewise.

In effect, we throw up our hands from the standpoint of planning and control of pure and fundamental research. But there are other areas in the research and development department of a company which do lend themselves to management planning and control.

Applied Research

In the field of applied research, periodic evaluation and planning is possible. But this requires that applied research be considered as a completely separate operation from that of pure and fundamental research. Before applied research can be planned, however, top management must go through some soul searching. It makes no sense to have an applied research department unless management has defined what research is trying to do in detail. Research plans must be integrated with company objectives. First, the company should determine what technology it really needs. This decision encompasses such basic problems as: What business does it want to be in? What is the desired rate of growth? What is the direction of growth desired? What percentage of the market is wanted? What is the profit ratio that is considered most desirable?

After getting some answers on questions such as these, the next problem is whether the research organization is an efficient one. We shall discuss this question later.

The third question is whether or not the present operation is yielding results.

And the fourth question: Is management actually using the results that have been obtained by the applied research department?

In talking of objectives, perhaps a down-to-earth example would be helpful. An automobile company might first decide that one of its major needs is a new automatic transmission. After a little thought it might be determined that the best automatic transmission to develop should be one that is useful in a low-horsepower automobile. A further requirement that such a transmission be competitive in cost with the standard gearshift could then be added. If on top of all this is added the requirement that this be developed within three years, we have a fairly practical applied research problem.

Given the problem, planning can begin. In a relatively short time, key people in the research department should be able to determine whether the project is feasible. Once they have determined that it *is* feasible, they should be able to project time and costs for completion. After management reviews these projections and discusses the whole problem with the research head, a reasonable budget should be determined, which in effect is a quantitative expression of the company's plan. As research on the project progresses, the costs can be compared with those projected, and any major variation should come to management's attention.

By lining up a number of projects in this same manner, with approximations of times and costs to complete, a forward-thinking management can evaluate each and determine which should be started immediately, which should be deferred, and which should be discarded. Obviously, the company's needs, and where it plans to go will have a great deal to do with the decision made.

One of business's chief problems in the research area is the measurement of research. How do we determine how good it is? Broadly speaking, this has been done in two ways: quantitative and qualitative. The typical quantitative approach for the evaluation of research uses mathematical formulas of one kind or another, and considers such factors as the following:

1. Profits on new or improved products
2. Profits obtained through cost reduction whether it be changing processes, methods, or raw materials
3. Savings on royalty payments
4. Royalties received from others
5. General good will obtained—public relations value

Quantitative analysis of research attempts to evaluate all these things against the cost of each program involved. Such evaluation is helpful in considering what has been done in the past, but it is certainly no guide as to what should happen in the future.

Those who favor qualitative measurement insist that the only way to evaluate a research operation is by broad management judgment. They talk about getting the "feel" of the situation. Actually what they are saying is that they feel no objective judgment can be made, but that a good subjective judgment based on confidence in an individual or individuals must be used. Certainly in the early phases of a new program, where nothing useful has been accomplished, any evaluation must depend upon confidence or lack of confidence in the department and its head as such.

Once an applied research department has been under way for a period of time, however, a combination of the quantitative and qualitative approach to evaluation of results can be extremely productive. Such questions as, "Did the department meet its time-table and cost schedule on a given project?" and "What actual profits have resulted in relation to total costs?" can be most helpful. In effect, use of the quantitative approach may be helpful in producing qualitative judgments.

Development

The businessman should feel at home in the development phase. Development is a business. Timetables and budgets should be realistic, and the man who can consistently produce on schedule at the costs outlined should do well. Let us not understate the degree of competence in engineering that must be present in a good development department. From observations, however, if a development department presents to top management a number of items that may be worked on, with clear-cut statements of production time needed, costs involved, and benefits anticipated, management is in a position to determine what should be undertaken now, with at least an approximation of the costs and potential benefits involved.

Decisions in the area of product development cannot be based on what a company can afford at a given time. An industry-by-industry review would indicate that the varying products produced tend to have a fairly definite life span. Most products are eventually superseded by other better, or seemingly better, products which are the result of someone's product development. Planning for and controlling product development is a basic responsibility of top management.

Summary

Research and development is not the vast uncharted field generally supposed. By using a segmented approach, and evaluating each project before it is undertaken, the areas of applied research and development can be run as businesses. There are no strict financial guidelines for pure and fundamental research. Nor should part of the research and development operation be tied to anticipated or past sales, profits, or any other measure. Many companies must do some applied research and development, merely to maintain their position. The future leaders are probably doing the most at this point. How much must be done can be determined only by a knowledge of what competitors in any given industry are doing. In the pure and fundamental research fields, research should be considered an investment, and the amount to be put into research should be considered in the light of alternative uses of capital by the company. A great deal of money has been poured down the drain because it has been invested in incompetent research staffs. If a company can develop evaluation techniques so that the competence of its research department can be assured, there can hardly be a better investment. Certainly a major part of corporate planning is, now, and will be for some time to come, research and development.

9 Administrative Costs

Outside the marketing, production, and research areas are certain other business functions, which are handled by staff and overhead departments. These administrative functions include accounting, finance, personnel, legal, and public relations. In very large companies, such functions as purchasing, traffic, and advertising may also have sizable representation at the corporate staff level.

The administrative departments, including the corporate officers and their staffs, tend to proliferate at an alarming rate, chiefly because no concerted, reasonable attempt to control them is made. Many managements, convinced that these areas do not lend themselves to objective control, tend to slash them arbitrarily when business is bad and allow them to burgeon when business is good.

A dispassionate analysis of administrative personnel, however, readily separates them into two groups: those working on desirable programs or projects (for example, preparation of a personnel recruiting booklet) and those engaged in activities which are essential to a company's existence (for example, paying bills).

In both groups are people whose work is essentially creative, while others are primarily occupied with mechanical tasks (that is, clerical and repetitive). A personnel director, for example, should function primarily in a creative fashion, while a file clerk in the same department is typically performing routine tasks.

Most administrative costs tend to fluctuate directly with the numbers of people involved. Such fixed expenses as rent, light, and heat, of course, are not affected by minor variations in departmental staffing. But, in general, a department such as public relations is likely to spend and to cost almost twice as much if it has six men instead of three. Such items as salaries, fringe benefits, office equipment, and even expense accounts vary directly with the number of people involved.

Thus, the best accounting controls for administrative costs must consider budgets for head counts as well as dollars.

Program Budgeting

Some of our best-run companies insist, at time of budget preparation, on program budgets from each administrative supervisor. In effect, these program budgets justify the jobs of all the people in each department by outlining as separate projects all areas of major activity with supporting detail covering the needed personnel and costs.

Evaluating which projects are worthwhile and should be continued can only be accomplished if management knows what is being done, and at what costs.

Analysis of one company's college recruiting program, for example, showed that 93 per cent of its recruits over the preceding eight years came from 40 per cent of the schools visited. When this came to light, the college recruiting department was cut by three men (50 per cent) with no noticeable loss in number or quality of recruits.

In another case a company found, on analysis of a program budget, that the equivalent of three full-time people in its public relations department were being employed clipping references to the company from periodicals. Investigation showed that this job could be handled by an outside clipping bureau at about 25 per cent of the cost, with better coverage.

By asking for program budgets from all administrative supervisors, management accomplishes two ends: it learns what jobs are being done, and how much each will cost. It can decide which jobs are worthwhile and which can be dispensed with. When a program budget is approved, the supervisor has both a mandate and ground rules as to how many people he should have and in what activities they should be engaged.

Repetitive Tasks

In a typical company, about three-fourths of the staff jobs are basically repetitive and even clerical, as opposed to the one-fourth that are creative. Despite this fact, it is the rare company that has a sound plan for staffing and controlling clerical costs.

Surveys and my own experience both indicate that the average office worker is productively employed only about 60 per cent of the time. This is not because he is lazier than his factory counterpart, but rather that he is improperly loaded with work (that is, work is not organized so that there is always something productive to do) and that he has little idea of what is expected of him in a normal working day.

With the ever-increasing growth in the number of people employed in processing "paper work"—brought on by more government reports, more need for management information, and more complexity in business generally—the problem of controlling administrative personnel and cost is assuming major importance.

One of the most successful answers we have seen is to borrow a page from successful factory operation and control—measure the jobs to be done, assign work to individuals on a planned basis, and check performance against the established standards.

This approach to administrative-cost control can pay sizable dividends. In one company, for example, six girls were employed in the accounts payable department, each being responsible for a

section of the alphabet—one handled all vendors with names start-
ing with A–D, another E–I, etc. Overtime ran high and discounts
were sometimes missed because of delays in getting payments out.
After the work load was measured and production standards were
established, it was quite apparent that vendor fluctuation gave some
girls only three or four hours' work a day, while others might fall a
week or two behind. When the operation was reorganized on
a scientific basis, only four girls were needed to keep on top of the
job. In this case, the staff was reduced by one-third, overtime was
eliminated, and all discounts are now being taken on time.

This is not an unusual situation. To an untrained eye, no one can
look as busy as a white collar worker who has all day to do two
hours' worth of work. The only answer is to measure the work content of each job.

Techniques which have been used to measure administrative
jobs vary from simple ones to the extremely complex. We shall
discuss briefly the following widely used techniques: average actual,
random work sampling, time study, and motion analysis with
predetermined times.

Average Actual

Statistical analysis of work performed in previous periods can
be helpful in determining reasonable standards for office work.
Comparison of outputs of clerical employees engaged in the same
task can be interesting, if the period of observation is long enough.
Not only do wide variations in productivity show up between individuals, but the work of each individual may show wide variations
in output on different days.

In establishing standards on the basis of historical average-actual
output, be careful to select the performances of competent workers
who had an adequate work load and who also tend to perform at
a normal (neither speeded nor slowed) pace.

The methods used to compute these standards build in allowances for rest periods, personal time, and fatigue, so that the stand-

ards developed represent performance which is attainable at a 100 per cent (or normal) activity level—if the work load is properly organized.

Obviously, standards set by using the average-actual technique will not be completely accurate; but if this procedure enables a company to raise its over-all clerical productive rate from 60 to even 90 per cent, the usefulness of this tool should be apparent. Moreover, use of this technique can enable a company to forecast personnel needs with fair accuracy, using changing work loads as a base.

Random Work Sampling

Applying statistical sampling to determine work content can vary widely in complexity. Although "ratio-delay" studies are only one utilization of the technique, the term has come to be broadly used by those who prefer to keep cost controls shrouded in mysticism. Essentially the work-sampling technique requires making random observations, observing statistical laws in number, to determine what is being done and how much of the total time available is spent on each of the observed activities.

A department head was once asked to share his secretary with another, newly appointed department head. The first gentleman, after checking with his secretary, declared that she had a full-time job, and hence could not be shared. An analyst kept a notebook record of a thousand random observations of the secretary over a four-week period, checking either "work" or "no work," depending on what the secretary was doing when observed. The results showed that the secretary was productively working only 27 per cent of the time. She now works for two men and both are well satisfied with the arrangement. This is the simplest kind of work sampling.

In another instance, an engineering department was studied at the request of top management, because of requisitions for more engineers than management "intuitively" felt were needed. Here, use of a technique involving complicated task identification showed that more than 50 per cent of so-called "engineering time" was being spent on drafting and other technician-type work, which could have been done by less skilled personnel at much lower rates than the average engineer's salary.

True random sampling can be extremely complex, involving the use of random number tables and a wide variety of performance classifications. Our purpose here is merely to point out that sampling has been and can be useful in controlling administrative costs.

Time Study

In many cases, the time-honored factory "stand-by," the stop watch, is the most practical answer to job measurement. Work standards can be established within very accurate boundaries, quickly and economically, by an experienced time-study man.

The greatest problem in time study, factory or office, is establishing the "level" of performance of the operator being observed. This requires that the analyst judge the skill and effort of the operator, then mentally compare it with a preconceived concept of normal performance. A fair amount of training is necessary before an analyst can judge the performance of an operator he is observing consistently—and consistent judgment of all jobs analyzed is essential.

Once the concept of good "leveling" has been established, the rest of the time-study technique is relatively simple to describe. An experienced time-study man observes one or more operators performing a task, records the time elapsed, and judges the level(s) of the performance. Based on repeated observations (the number of which depend upon the complexity of the job and the amount of accuracy desired), the standard, or "should take" time, is set. Clerks are then "loaded" (that is, given work to be done in a stated period) based on this should-take time. Evaluation of performance against standards then forms the basis for judging employees, supervisors, and budget requests.

Motion Analysis with Predetermined Times

Setting standards by use of predetermined time values is probably the most accurate, albeit the most costly, method. This technique involves the use of basic time data which have been developed over the years by people active in this field. Among the most frequently used data tables are:

BMT (Basic Motion Timestudy)—developed by Bailey and Presgrave of Woods, Gordon and Company of Toronto
WF (Work Factor)—developed by Quick, Shea and O'Brien, at Philco and RCA
MTM (Methods-Time Measurement)—developed by Maynard, Stegemarten and Schwab, at the Methods Engineering Council

Data tables in book form are available for each of these.

Each system varies in the application of detail, but the basic approach is the same. The standard time for any clerical operation is built up by analyzing each of the many separate motions involved and then applying the proper standard time value to each motion. As a simple example, picking up a pencil and writing a figure in a certain place might easily entail as many as fifteen separate actions (reach, grasp, pre-position, move, align, assemble, etc.). A time standard can be prepared by adding the predetermined time for each of these motions to transition times, where required. The sum total of these times is the standard time for the entire operation.

The amount of time that it takes to set standards by this method is manifest. Hence, predetermined times are most used in setting standards when the jobs measured are very repetitive and involve a number of people—in situations where 2 to 5 per cent improvement can mean substantial dollar savings.

Summary

Planning and control of administrative costs by use of accounting has not been adequately developed by most businesses. The key-

stones are the use of a *project budget,* which involves making qualitative decisions as to whether projects are worthwhile, with full
knowledge of quantitative factors (costs—basically people); and the
measurement of all repetitive and clerical operations so that the
numbers of people actually needed to do the job are clearly and
objectively defined. It is often practical to set standards for clerical
performance even when some employees handle fifteen to twenty
different tasks each day. Companies following measurement programs in the paperwork areas have been able to reduce clerical
costs from 20 to 40 per cent.

In effect, the lowest level of supervision (the "first-line supervisor") in the so-called "overhead" departments can be measured
and held accountable for what he does. First, he has specific goals
and project budgets. Second, he has the facts and figures necessary
to determine how many people are needed at varying levels of
activity. The same standards that he uses are being used by management. As a result, "communication problems" about budgets cease
to exist. The requirement that he account for the use of his people's
time forces him to balance work force with prevailing work load.
Finally, his people are happier—because they know what is expected of them.

10   Capital Budgeting

Capital budgeting has received increasing attention from business analysts in recent years. Unfortunately, much of their work, because of its complexity, has made relatively little impact on most businesses.

Every business has capital budgeting problems, whether it uses this term or not. Such questions as whether and when to replace machinery and equipment, build new plants, add a new product line, and even invest in research are all capital budgeting decisions.

Many businessmen say, with some validity, that decisions on how to invest money are beset with so many imponderables (for example, what competition will do, how customer demands may change, and how technology will develop) that it matters little what methods of evaluating desirability of alternative choices are used. They argue that the good executive will be so familiar with all facets of his business that he will intuitively consider risk factors and potential gains and come up with better answers than any formula might provide. However, examination of executive decisions in such a simple area as truck replacements demonstrates that many experienced executives make unwise decisions which could be avoided if they gave a little more attention to theory.

The plea that "you cannot tell what is going to happen in the future, so you rely on intuition" ignores the fact that, even for a manager with both background and prescience, an organized approach to where money should be spent can help in decision making.

Further, as operations expand, top management becomes further removed from specifics, and cannot rely on its own knowledge of each situation.

Ranking of Alternative Investments

Since most businesses do not have limitless funds on which to draw and since there are many alternative uses for money, some method of ranking projects in order of desirability is needed. In discussing ranking, we shall consider only investments for which both the resources used and benefits to be received can be expressed in terms of dollars. Alternative uses of executive time are, in a real sense, investment decisions, but they are beyond the scope of this book. On the other side of the picture, investments made to improve employee morale or to cut accident rates are valid, but since they seldom can be expressed in dollars, we shall not dwell on them.

Broadly speaking, there are three types of alternative investments: mutually exclusive, dependent, and independent investments. Each will be briefly discussed.

Mutually Exclusive Investments

Investments are said to be mutually exclusive when the undertaking of one investment rules out the others under consideration. For example, in designing a plant, many of the alternatives are mutually exclusive, such as the use of gas, steam, or electrical power. Selection of the site for a new plant also involves the several mutually exclusive investments.

The ranking of mutually exclusive investments in order to choose the best one offers one potential pitfall. Suppose, for example, you face the choice of spending (1) $5,000 for a machine which will produce a saving of $5,000 each year for the next five years, or (2) $10,000 for a machine which will produce a saving of $7,500 a year for the next five years. Almost any ranking system, including those discussed later in this chapter, will indicate that choice 1 is preferable to choice 2. If, however, you look at choice 2 on an incremental basis, it can be seen that by spending an additional $5,000 you will return an additional $2,500 a year. Assuming no alternative uses for this additional $5,000 that would bring about as high a rate of return, choice 2 might well be the better one.

Dependent Investments

Investments are dependent if one depends upon another, as in the case of an attachment for a piece of machinery. If the piece of machinery were not in existence, obviously there would be no need for the attachment. Deciding to build a plant raises a number of prime examples of dependent investments. The type of equipment to be bought, the design of the building, and many other items become dependent investment decisions.

Major investment decisions are usually accompanied by a host of dependent decisions complementary to the initial one.

Independent Investments

An independent investment is one which stands on its own feet and which may be undertaken whether or not any other investment is made. Sometimes, because of lack of cash, a company is forced to choose between a number of investments; but as long as available cash is the only limiting factor, such investments are termed independent ones. Some examples of independent investments are the purchase of a warehouse, expansion of a plant, and tooling up to add a new product to the line.

General Considerations

In brief, establishment of ranking in order of desirability, keeping in mind the problem of interdependency, is essential if available cash is to be most wisely spent.

Ranking should also be done on a completely heterogeneous basis, mixing in order of desirability such possibilities as lease or buy problems, size of plant, refunding of debt, and the many replacement questions that arise.

Business as a whole is not ignorant of this problem. For some years, various methods of investigating alternative uses of capital have been employed, but some of these have been of more harm than help. Specifically, the two most popular tests have been the "payback period" and the "rate of return." The fallacies will be pointed out as each of these methods is explored.

Payback Period

Although wide variations exist in detailed application of this test, the theory is essentially simple. The question is, How long will it take to get back the amount invested, through savings or increased profits? One major oil company, for example, will not consider any investment that will not "pay back" in three years.

Some of the major variations in defining how payback is figured are:

1. Is amount invested the gross amount or is it the net after salvage recovered in the transaction?

2. Should the total investment be considered, or only the equity portion? In other words, should a different approach be taken if a substantial portion of the money to be invested comes from borrowings?

3. Should the gain to be made be figured before or after income taxes?

4. Should depreciation be considered in calculating the gain, and, if so, on what basis?*

5. Should interest on borrowed capital be considered an element of cost in computing gain?

These questions are cited merely to point out that the payback theory is not just theory but a term which covers the division of some kind of investment figure by some sort of gain figure to get a time period over which the investment will be paid back.

To point out some of the problems inherent in using the payback system of evaluating capital investments, let us consider three examples. In each case, we may assume for the sake of simplicity that $10,000 is required, that the item has a ten-year life, that depreciation will be considered on a straight-line basis (10 per cent a year), that there is no salvage value involved, that gain is measured on an after-tax basis, and that we are not considering interest on borrowed capital as a cost. Further, payback has been computed on the basis of earnings, rather than cash.

Example I

ASSUMED FACTS. A new machine may be bought for $10,000 which will result in gross operating savings of $21,000 in the first year by eliminating a bottleneck in producing a new product. After the first year, however, the new machine offers no advantage over present equipment, which is adequate to handle expected volume.

CALCULATION

Gross savings in first year	$21,000
Less depreciation at 10%	1,000
Savings in first year before taxes	$20,000
Income taxes rounded to 50%	10,000
Net after-tax saving first year	$10,000
Number of years to pay back original investment: 1	

* Federal income tax law allows the use of straight-line depreciation, declining-balance method, or sum-of-the-digits method. Each of these methods may result in markedly different depreciation costs in any given year.

Example II

ASSUMED FACTS. A new machine may be bought for $10,000 which will produce gross operating savings of $6,000 per year for the foreseeable future.

CALCULATION

Gross savings each year	$6,000
Less depreciation	1,000
Savings before taxes	$5,000
Income taxes rounded to 50%	2,500
Net savings each year	$2,500

Number of years to pay back
original investment: 4

Example III

ASSUMED FACTS. A still different machine may be bought for $10,000 which, because of complex "break-in" problems, will produce only $1,000 in gross savings the first year, $3,000 in the second year, $5,000 the third year, and $8,000 per year thereafter.

CALCULATION

	1st Yr.	2d Yr.	3d Yr.	Each Year Thereafter
Gross savings	$1,000	$3,000	$5,000	$8,000
Less depreciation	1,000	1,000	1,000	1,000
Savings before taxes		$2,000	$4,000	$7,000
Income taxes @ 50%		1,000	2,000	3,500
Net savings		$1,000	$2,000	$3,500

Number of years to pay back
original investment: 5

These examples are oversimplified, but they demonstrate the basic weaknesses of the payback system. Following the payback theory to the letter, these three alternative investments have been presented in order of desirability: Example I showed a one-year payback; Example II showed a four-year payback; and Example III showed a five-year payback. These simple examples permit us to cut through the theory and see that Example I is the least desirable, in that we are merely trading dollars. Further, there is a possibility that Example III may be more desirable than Example II over the long pull.

The weaknesses of the payback theory, then, are that gains made after the payback period are not taken into account and timing of gains is not considered.

Rate of Return

Somewhat less in vogue, but still frequently used, is the "rate of return" theory. It is subject to the same basic variations as the payback theory, plus some additional ones.

The rate-of-return procedure attempts to measure the gain from a capital investment against the amount invested, in percentage terms, so that the answer is, in effect, the rate of return on the money spent. There are several variations of this method, including the first-year return, total return, and average annual return.

In computing the *first-year return,* the net gain of the first year is figured as a percentage of the total investment. In figuring *total return,* total proceeds over the life of the item are computed as a percentage of the total investment. The calculation of *average annual return* is similar to total return, except that it is reduced to an annual basis.

These three variations, when applied to the three examples presented earlier in this chapter, give the results shown in Table 10–1.

TABLE 10–1

Example	1st Yr. Return	Total Return	Average Annual Return
I	100%	100%	10%
II	25	250	25
III		275	27.5

These examples indicate clearly that *first-year return* is inadequate, for once again Example I comes out with the highest rank, despite the fact that it represents only "swapping dollars." As in the payback theory, no consideration is given to *total* gains from investment.

Total return and *average annual return* offer the decided advantage of consideration of total proceeds. The big weakness in these methods is that they give no weight to the timing of proceeds. Later in this chapter, I shall discuss the fact that a dollar returned in the first year of operation is worth more than that same dollar returned in the fifth year of operation.

To make any valid appraisal of a potential investment, some consideration of this concept of "future worth" or "present value" must be included.

Present-value Concepts

A graphic example of present-value concepts was set forth in a letter addressed to a major magazine* as follows:

While New York is a most fascinating metropolis, the legendary Indian who sold it for $24 was a pretty sharp salesman too.

If he had put his $24 away at 6% interest, compounded semiannually, it would now be over $9.5 billion, and could buy most if not all of the land back. If he had been trader enough to get 6½%, it would now be $48.6 billion, and could buy the land plus improvements. At 7%—which some borrowers now pay—it would have grown to $245 billion, and could buy New York State complete; or almost make the Federal Government solvent!

S. BRANCH WALKER
Stamford, Connecticut

This is an extreme example, of course, but no method of evaluating alternative capital investments is valid unless some consideration is given to present value of future money.

The phrase "present value of future money" may be confusing at first glance, but it represents an important concept. It means that

* Printed in part in *Life,* August 31, 1959.

$1.00 in hand right now is worth more than a promise, no matter how valid, to pay $1.00 at some point in the future. The reason is that money in hand can be used for alternative, profitable purposes. At minimum, the $1.00 in hand could be put in a savings bank, fully insured, and draw interest at 5 per cent. Always available to us, this $1.00 would be worth $1.28 if the interest were compounded quarterly for the next five years.

The company possessing an unlimited supply of capital resources is rare. If such a company exists and keeps its cash in a checking account, drawing no interest, the present-value concept is not applicable. On the other hand, the board of directors of such a company might draw severe censure for not doing something with its excess money that will make a profit.

Typically, companies have more possible alternatives for the use of cash than they have cash. If this were not true, the whole concept of "ranking," previously discussed in this chapter, would have no value.

Much of our discussion so far has been negative, showing the weaknesses of capital budgeting concepts that do not take into consideration this concept of present value of future money. Present value is a very important, valid concept which is frequently overlooked.

It might seem that the rate to be applied in discounting future dollars could be universally established at the same rate for all, but this is not true. The drawback to the use of present-value methods is that no two experts agree as to what a proper discount is in any given situation.

Two major factors enter into the determination of the proper rate for discounting future funds. These are the degree of risk involved and the cost of capital. The investor in government bonds, for example, might well evaluate comparable investments in terms of a 4 per cent discount rate. The oil "wildcatter," on the other hand, might well discount future dollars at 30 per cent or more.

If funds are being borrowed for purposes of capital investment, the "floor" on the discount rate is the amount of interest being paid on the borrowings. In this case some risk factor should be added to the interest rate.

One school of thought argues that the cost of capital is the average return on equity (net income divided by total stockholders' equity); hence, this is the figure at which future dollars should be discounted. The theory here is that the money currently at work in the business is earning at this rate, so that no alternative investments should be considered which do not bring this rate of return. The foolishness of this theory is patent when one considers the make-up of the assets on a balance sheet. No weight is given to management talents and customer good will. Frequently asset values of plant and equipment are stated way below replacement costs. The use of return on equity as the cost of capital is often unrealistic. An advertising or publishing company, for example, may well earn 50 per cent on equity on the average. To make a decision on replacement of an accounting machine, for example, using a 50 per cent discount rate, is absurd. In short, selection of the proper discount rate is a complex subject.

A simple, workable solution to this problem is for each company to establish a basic cost-of-capital factor, which is then weighted by a varying risk factor for each investment considered. If, for example, money may be borrowed at 6 per cent, a proposal to replace equipment for use on a staple product might well be evaluated using an 8 per cent discount rate, thus adding only a 2 per cent risk factor. This same company, however, might evaluate an investment for tooling up for a new product at a 15 or 20 per cent discount rate, using in this instance a risk factor of 9 to 14 per cent.

Those who are searching for the will-o'-the-wisp—an automatic ranking system which eliminates all managerial judgment—may say that this proposal adds nothing and that we may as well use the time-honored intuition by which many fortunes have been made. This I vigorously deny. The final word on capital budgeting has not yet come, but at least we have a system for evaluating like risks and putting varying risks in quantitative terms so that some reasoned judgment may be applied.

Let us assume, for example, that our three previously described examples of equipment replacement are to be discounted at 8 per cent to see which is preferable. The initial investment of $10,000 in each case will result in the present values shown in Table 10–2.

TABLE 10–2*

Example	1st Yr.	2d Yr.	3d Yr.	4th Yr.	5th Yr.	10-Yr. Total
I	$10,185					$10,185
II	3,241	$3,001	$2,728	$2,573	$2,383	23,485
III	926	1,715	2,381	3,308	3,063	23,610

* All figures are taken from standard data tables prepared to show present values of $1 at 8 per cent. All costs have been assumed to be direct (unallocated) and depreciation has been added back.

If we believe these results, we find that Examples II and III are about equally desirable, and Example I, as we saw by inspection earlier, is not worth entering into (since it merely trades dollars). It should also be apparent that, as our assumed cost of capital rises above 8 per cent, Example II becomes increasingly desirable compared with Example III.

Practical Examples

Some examples of the use of capital budgeting, and, more specifically, present value concepts may now be helpful.

Example A: Choice of Alternatives

Let us assume that we have a choice of Machine I or Machine II, either of which can do a specific job for a company equally well. The assumed facts are shown in Table 10–3.

The total discounted cost for Machine I over the 3-year period at a rate of 10 per cent is $1,834, or $611 per year. The total discounted cost for Machine II over the 6-year period at the same 10 per cent rate is $3,431, or $572 per year. Based upon this calculation, it would appear that our best buy is Machine II. A closer look,

TABLE 10–3

	Machine I	Machine II
Life	3 years	6 years
Price	$1,000	$2,000
Operating cost:		
1st year	200	100
2d year	400	200
3d year	600	300
4th year		400
5th year		500
6th year		600
Salvage value	300	200

however, reveals that, in the case of Machine I, we have not figured in the cost of the second 3-year period.

In short, if we figure on replacing Machine I at the end of 3 years, still using the 10 per cent discount rate, we find that for the 6-year period the discounted cost of Machine I comes to $3,212, or $535 per year, clearly the "best buy."

The reason this example turns out this way should be obvious—the company has available an extra $1,000 for three years to use for some other purpose.

Example B: Comparison with Existing Conditions

One company, entranced with the essential common sense and simplicity involved in the use of the present-value concept, replaced four delivery trucks of comparable size with four new trucks. The trucks replaced were four, seven, ten, and twelve years old, respectively. The justification reports (required to justify all capital expenditures) showed annual over-all savings ranging from $500 for replacing the 4-year-old truck to $2,500 on the 12-year-old truck.

One possible conclusion is that only the oldest trucks should have been replaced because of the greater savings involved. To carry this further, the longer you wait in replacing trucks, the more money you save when you replace them.

If the amount of cash available is severely limited, you might well replace only the oldest trucks at any given time; but we now see the prime argument for ranking investment opportunities. Replacement of the newest truck may net the company more profit than other items in which investments might normally be made.

Summary

A brief chapter such as this does not purport to be the definitive answer to capital budgeting. Some minor technical points have been disregarded in order to establish a basic point of view.

Some businesses approach capital budgeting by deciding how much they can spend over a given period and then lining up items in order of desirability until the total amount is committed. Others, with more cash available, decide which items are desirable based on some formula, and then commit for all proposals that qualify under that formula. Neither of these approaches is necessarily bad, if some consistent method is used in evaluating the desirability of the various proposals for spending money.

Any business has many potential uses for its available capital. Of course, no technique can rank all possible uses of money—for example, how does one rank the value of a new ball field for employee recreation? At the same time, a consistent technique for ranking investment alternatives can lend objectivity to management judgments which have been basically subjective to date.

The big problem in evaluating alternative investments is not the formula to be used, but the reliability of the assumptions made. The best formula in the world will be worthless if the figures used are invalid. The real time-consuming efforts in any capital budgeting operation lie in getting the facts or best estimates available. How much will a new machine save in each year? What are potential sales of the new product if it is added to the line? Getting reliable answers to questions such as these—information needed before any formula can be applied—requires a combination of hard work and good business judgment.

Once the best assumptions and underlying facts are at hand, the application of a formula for ranking is not time-consuming. The statistical application of the present-value concept is relatively easy, once the discount for each project is established.

The rate of discount to be used is made up of two factors: the cost of capital and the degree of risk involved. The cost of capital for a given company at a particular time should be viewed as a constant figure. Arriving at what this figure should be is not easy, and no universal formula for determining cost of capital exists. Once such a figure is agreed upon, however, the risk factor for each potential is arrived at and added to the cost of capital to provide varying discount rates for the different potential investments. Applying these discount rates to the investment possibilities will result in discounted dollar figures, which furnish the information necessary to rank the alternatives in order of desirability.

It is my firm belief that no technique is about to replace judgment. For instance, in the procedure outlined above, judgment enters heavily into the determination of assumptions on each project, the establishment of the cost of capital, and the degree of risk involved in each situation. At the same time, a consistently applied technique that includes the present-value concept will provide specific quantitative help in reaching judgments and will tend to bring into line widely divergent conclusions on the same matter by different people.

11   Cash Management

To the manager who is not trained in accounting, a prime source of confusion is the difference between cash and profit. Most of our readers are certainly sophisticated enough to recognize that a retailer can sell all his goods below cost, not pay his suppliers, and have a substantial amount of money in the till. As a matter of fact, some successful bankruptcies have come about in precisely this manner.

Having an adequate amount of cash, however, is essential for any business. Good cash management is of increasing importance in today's economic climate, with its ever-increasing demands for growth, new products, and expansion, coupled with increasing interest rates. In addition to planning and control for profits, the businessman must construct his plans and operate his business with an eye to what cash he will need and when, and he must be prepared to meet these needs. Some otherwise successful businesses have floundered, despite good profit showings, because they lacked cash when it was needed. Even more businesses have found that they could not keep up with competition in building new, more efficient facilities, because of lack of cash.

The four essentials of an effective cash-management program are these:

1. Plan cash requirements ahead for a number of years. This can lead to the development of appropriate sources which you can tap through borrowings or equity sales, as needed.

2. Reduce cash balances carried for "emergencies" or "contingencies." Such balances often result from lack of planning. These monies should be put to work to earn more money for your company.

3. Make sure that all money is always working. Even seasonally high cash balances, which may result from the nature of certain businesses, are indefensible in that your money is an asset and should be out working for you if you do not need it immediately in your business.

4. Plan ahead if more money will be needed on a seasonal basis. Your "friendly" banker will be more impressed and hence more friendly if he knows well in advance how much money you will need, when you will need it, and when you will repay it. The preplanning approach can convince the banker that your needs are due to normal fluctuations in your business requirements rather than to financial weakness.

On pages 36–38, we discussed the statement of source and application of funds. This is a useful statement of what has happened to cash in the immediate past. But equally essential is cash planning for the future.

Figure 11–1 demonstrates the flow of cash in a typical business. We receive cash from the liquidation of accounts receivable (money owed us); we receive goods from suppliers which we turn into cash and then use to repay the suppliers; the bank lends us cash which must be repaid; and the long-suffering stockholder gives us cash on which he expects to receive a return.

Cash is paid out for several purposes. Some money is used for research and development; and assuming that this department develops worthwhile products, substantial sums of money are put into plant and raw materials and labor to produce the products.

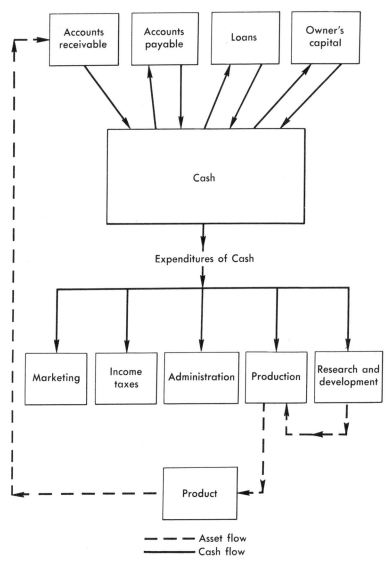

Sources of Cash

Accounts receivable   Accounts payable   Loans   Owner's capital

Cash

Expenditures of Cash

Marketing   Income taxes   Administration   Production   Research and development

Product

— — — Asset flow
——— Cash flow

Figure 11–1

We also must pay executives, secretaries, office boys, etc. And we also pay for advertising, promotion, and salesmen who sell the product. Assuming we do well, we must pay income taxes. The sales of all our products end up as accounts receivable (money due from customers), and we then start the whole cash process over again.

To understand control of the cash cycle, let us discuss these three aspects of the situation: the cash budget, the improving of cash availability, and financial management.

The Cash Budget

In building up a cash budget, one must first prepare a profit and loss budget in fairly conventional form. Projected sales are converted into planned inventory levels and production schedules. With this data available, the company's cash budget can be prepared. Although the budget can be prepared in the form of a statement of source and application of funds, it is more useful in the form of a statement of cash receipts and disbursements (see Table 11–1) because this statement deals more specifically with cash movements and their timing. If your cash receipts and disbursements statements show a relatively even flow throughout the year, your cash availability problem should be considerably less than if, as is more common, there are wide swings throughout the year in your need for cash.

Actual cash flow should then be reported in comparison to the plan. The forecast may have been prepared by quarter, month, week, or day, and the reports to management should be in the same detail. Normally, the more critical the cash position, the greater the need for detailed and frequent reporting.

Improving Cash Availability

An advantage in preparing a cash budget is that by giving attention to cash, you tend to find ways to improve cash availability. Some areas which can be improved are discussed below.

TABLE 11-1

ABC COMPANY
Statement of Projected Cash Receipts and Disbursements
For the year ended May 31, 19—

Receipts	June	July	August	September	October	November	December	January	February	March	April	May
Accounts receivable at beginning of month	$562,000	$561,000	$573,000	$574,000	$599,000	$606,000	$600,000	$585,000	$624,000	$616,000	$629,000	$597,000
Gross sales	324,000	337,000	333,000	358,000	354,000	345,000	333,000	378,000	354,000	370,000	333,000	341,000
	$886,000	$898,000	$906,000	$932,000	$953,000	$951,000	$933,000	$963,000	$978,000	$986,000	$962,000	$938,000
Accounts receivable at end of month	561,000	573,000	574,000	599,000	606,000	600,000	585,000	624,000	616,000	629,000	597,000	592,000
	$325,000	$325,000	$332,000	$333,000	$347,000	$351,000	$348,000	$339,000	$362,000	$357,000	$365,000	$346,000
Refund of prior year's federal income tax							20,000					
Total receipts	$325,000	$325,000	$332,000	$333,000	$347,000	$351,000	$368,000	$339,000	$362,000	$357,000	$365,000	$346,000

	1	2	3	4	5	6	7	8	9	10	11	12
Disbursements												
Direct material	$140,000	$138,000	$148,000	$146,000	$143,000	$138,000	$156,000	$146,000	$153,000	$138,000	$141,000	$152,000
Payroll	115,000	112,000	120,000	119,000	116,000	112,000	120,000	119,000	125,000	112,000	115,000	124,000
Indirect materials, supplies, payroll taxes, and services	30,000	29,000	31,000	31,000	30,000	29,000	33,000	31,000	32,000	29,000	30,000	32,000
Commissions	23,000	22,000	24,000	24,000	23,000	22,000	25,000	24,000	25,000	22,000	23,000	25,000
Discounts and freight	13,000	13,000	14,000	14,000	13,000	13,000	15,000	14,000	14,000	13,000	13,000	14,000
Bonus							7,000					
Expenditure for plant modernization program				8,000								
Total disbursements	$321,000	$314,000	$337,000	$342,000	$325,000	$314,000	$356,000	$334,000	$349,000	$314,000	$322,000	$347,000
Excess of Receipts (Disbursements)	$ 4,000	$ 11,000	($ 5,000)	($ 9,000)	$ 22,000	$ 37,000	$ 12,000	$ 5,000	$ 13,000	$ 43,000	$ 43,000	($ 1,000)
Cash balance at beginning of month	111,000	105,000	106,000	91,000	72,000	84,000	111,000	113,000	108,000	111,000	144,000	177,000
	$115,000	$116,000	$101,000	$ 82,000	$ 94,000	$121,000	$123,000	$118,000	$121,000	$154,000	$187,000	$176,000
Repayments of bank borrowings	10,000	10,000	10,000	10,000	10,000	10,000	10,000	10,000	10,000	10,000	10,000	46,000
Cash balance at end of month	$105,000	$106,000	$ 91,000	$ 72,000	$ 84,000	$111,000	$113,000	$108,000	$111,000	$144,000	$177,000	$130,000
Accumulated bank borrowings	$146,000	$136,000	$126,000	$116,000	$106,000	$ 96,000	$ 86,000	$ 76,000	$ 66,000	$ 56,000	$ 46,000	-0-

"ABC Company—Statement of Projected Cash Receipts and Disbursements" is reprinted with the permission of *The Journal of Accountancy*.

BILLING. It is axiomatic that the quicker bills get out, the sooner you get paid. Moreover, errors in billing result in delay in cash payments. The smooth flow of accurate bills on a timely basis can increase cash flow markedly.

PROCESSING CASH RECEIPTS. It is surprising how many companies do not deposit checks received until these receipts are posted to customer accounts receivable cards. Sometimes one questionable item may hold up a whole batch of deposits. In times of tight money, particularly, such practices are foolish. Checks should be deposited in the bank as soon as possible and problems in identifying differences should be resolved later.

BANK COLLECTION SERVICES. Many companies now use "lockbox" services, which are offered by most commercial banks and to which the customer remits directly. The bank opens the mail, deposits the cash, and gives its customer a detailed listing of the sources of funds deposited. This approach allows a company to use its funds before processing its remittances by crediting individual accounts receivable.

CONTROLLING BRANCH CASH. A company that receives cash at various locations should set up a system of remittances to a central point. Although local branches should have cash balances adequate to repay the banks for their services, these local balances often get out of control. It is simple to set up a minimum-maximum-balance policy for each location and to have automatic transfers made to and from the principal account, by wire if it is sufficiently important.

CASH DISCOUNT AND CREDIT. Periodically, a thorough review of cash-discount and credit policies can help improve cash receipts. Many people do not realize that a cash discount of 2 per cent for payment in thirty days is the equivalent of 24 per cent per annum. Whether a company needs to offer cash discounts to bring in money rapidly depends in part on industry practice, but in most industries the cash discount is disappearing. This puts even more pressure on improving credit policies, so that a company is on top of its accounts receivable at all times. Accounts in arrears need considerable attention from both the standpoint of collection efforts and the condition under which future shipments will be made.

VENDOR PAYMENTS. On the other side of the picture, there is no point in paying each bill as it arrives. In dealing with numerous suppliers, a brief study can determine the most advantageous way of paying each. If, for example, a supplier has a 2 per cent ten days, net thirty days policy, he should be paid on the tenth day. Other suppliers may have just a net thirty-day policy; their bills can be accumulated and paid once a month. In making payment decisions consider what money costs you. Then you can determine on what schedule your suppliers will be paid.

Financial Management

Since cash flow deals primarily with current assets and working capital, we will not deal here with problems of fulfilling long-term capital commitments except to point out that a company's ability to take advantage of short-term opportunities can be significantly increased if adequate long-term financing is already in the picture. In the short term, some of the policies which should be considered in connection with cash are described below.

FINANCING OF ACCOUNTS RECEIVABLE. We have discussed the need for collecting accounts receivable promptly. It is possible to turn these assets into cash as soon as the merchandise is shipped by obtaining loans from banks or factoring organizations or by selling the receivables to such organizations. These arrangements can be made without the customer's knowledge. Interest rates are typically quite high, however, on financing accounts receivable. Before entering into such an arrangement, it would be well to exhaust other avenues for obtaining cash.

CUSTOMER FINANCING. An approach common to the large appliance and automobile industries is called "floor planning." The manufacturer arranges with a finance company, possibly its own subsidiary, to provide its dealers with financing for floor stocks. This encourages the dealer to display the product where it can be sold and enables the manufacturer to move it out of his inventory more easily.

ACCOUNTS PAYABLE. Just as your own company will grant credit to make a sale, many vendors will extend credit, particularly to tide a customer over a seasonal peak. It is not unusual for a company in the fertilizer business, for example, to allow ninety days for payment to encourage dealers to stock up before the heavy selling season. Or, a large supplier with heavy borrowing capacity will often give special terms to smaller customers who lack that capacity. As a matter of fact, in some areas suppliers will give merchandisers goods "on consignment" and expect payment from their dealers only when a sale is made.

INVENTORIES. Inventories can be used as security for cash borrowings in much the same way as accounts receivable. Also, where products are being manufactured to special order, it is not unusual to arrange progress payments or cash advances to help cover the costs of work in process. Using customer-supplied materials is another form of advance which can sometimes be obtained.

Most companies, however, have too much money invested in inventory. A thorough review of inventory, then, can result in liquidation of substantial amounts, thus adding to their cash position. Increasing the frequency of turnover of a company's inventory can also have a dramatic effect on its cash requirements. Control techniques which evaluate a manager's performance in terms of return on investment can be of substantial aid in improving cash flow.

SALE AND LEASEBACKS. The conversion of plant, equipment, vehicles, and other assets to cash through a study of sale and leaseback possibilities has helped many companies improve their cash flow. A word of caution: Be sure to study economic and tax consequences plus the effect on the general credit of your organization.

EVALUATION OF CAPITAL INVESTMENTS. In Chapter 10, we discussed criteria for determining a capital investment policy. Certainly, any company's policy will be influenced by its present and prospective cash situation. In a period of cash "squeeze," a company might well cut back on capital investments which are expected to pay out only over the long term, while concentrating on investments which will bring in cash more quickly, even if less desirable over the long term.

INCOME TAX POLICIES. Income tax laws and regulations allow considerable variation in how various items may be accounted for in computing taxes due. For example, depreciation may be speeded up and certain research and development expenses may be immediately written off rather than capitalized. We only note here that the lower the net income reported for tax purposes, the less tax to be paid, and the more cash available to the taxpayer for other uses.

DISPOSITION OF IDLE ASSETS. We briefly referred to this in connection with inventories. However, there are other areas of a business, fixed assets for example, where a searching examination might establish that the conversion of the asset to cash, even at a loss, might be very desirable. Acknowledging a past mistake may be painful, but it is foolish to keep assets on hand in hope that a use for them will turn up. In some cases, this kind of review can provide substantial cash to be used in a productive manner.

USE OF IDLE CASH. Although having too much cash on hand at any given time is not as prevalent as it was ten or fifteen years ago, it still occurs in some companies. If there is substantial cash on hand to meet seasonal needs, there are two routes open. When the cash is not needed it can be invested in short-term securities which will result in repayment as needed. Or, the excess cash can be put into projects or facilities, and outside financing can be obtained to help meet peak needs. At any rate, it is no longer stylish for a corporate treasurer to point with pride to large cash balances as an indication of solidity and good management. Cash should be put to work.

Summary

There is real difference between cash and net profit. Cash is an essential tool which should be used wisely to help increase net profit. By planning and controlling cash through effective information feedback and action, a business can travel the road to growth and avoid setbacks.

PART III

Management Uses of Operations Research

12 Operations Research as a Planning Tool

It would be difficult to find any business subject that has created more excitement but is less understood than Operations Research (or systems analysis or management science—whatever one chooses to call it). Leading business periodicals have devoted much space to the subject over the past few years; yet few executives understand what this highly touted field consists of or how it can be helpful.

Operations Research has been badly oversold, and in many quarters it is misunderstood, shrouded in an unnecessary aura of mathematical formulas. Many leading early practitioners came from the halls of academe and apparently devoted their talents toward impressing one another rather than solving business problems. Operations Research is certainly not the answer to all the world's problems, or even those of business, but it does offer some helpful tools to aid the executive in planning and operating his business more effectively.

What Operations Research Is and Is Not

Operations Research is, very simply, research aimed at increasing the effectiveness of an organization's operations. It has been used, with genuine benefit, to provide better answers to such questions as these: How large should our inventories be? How much of our product should we make now? How should we allocate our manufacturing facilities among the products we make? Where should our warehouses be located? How much of our advertising should we put into newspapers, as opposed to magazines, radio, or TV? What size territories should our salesmen cover? How many salesmen should we have? What will happen if we lower or raise prices? What price should we bid on a specific contract? What will sales amount to next month? When should we replace our fleet of trucks? How can we best maintain quality control? These are just a few of the thousands of problems, the solution of which has been markedly assisted by the use of Operations Research. In brief, Operations Research attempts to supply meaningfully analyzed information on those "how," "when," and "what if" questions that were traditionally left to hunch, intuition, and hopeful guess. It is an approach to the analysis of a business's operations which enables the manager to improve his planning and control decisions.

Operations Research is not, and cannot become, a substitute for good management. Most attempts to create operational models for whole enterprises have failed miserably, because so many factors involved in making a business successful defy quantification. The success of a well-designed Operations Research project depends largely on the extent to which the factors considered can be set forth in *quantitative* terms; when a manager gets the Operations Research answer to a problem, he can then apply his *qualitative* judgment to come up with the right answer.

For example, we know of a company which could be made significantly more profitable by dropping certain product lines. However, the owner-management has said that it intends to carry these lines as long as it is in power. Operations Research can tell how much has been lost and how much is likely to be lost, but the decision to continue the lines, which may be well-founded and not merely emotional, must be made by management.

A major stumbling block to the understanding of Operations Research has been its frequent use of mathematical models in problem solving. Understanding the use of mathematical models—as opposed to the complex formula which can be applied to the model —is not difficult. For example, suppose you are standing at the curb preparing to cross the street. A car is approaching you from, say, about 60 feet away. You have a decision to make: Should you try to cross the street now or should you wait until the car passes? Assuming you are in a rush to get somewhere, your objective is to cross as quickly as possible without being struck down. Intuitively, whether you are conscious of it or not, your mind compares the time you think it will take to get out of the way of the oncoming car with the time you expect the car will take to pass you. Most people are able to make this sort of decision (with a varying safety factor called "caution") quite easily, and it doesn't seem to bother them that they have used a mathematical model in doing so.

A mathematical model is simply a set of relationships in quantitative terms that is used to represent a real world situation. In the automobile example the mathematical model consisted of the time we guessed each event would take.

Let us recognize quickly, however, that no mathematical model can consider all qualitative nuances such as your state of mind when you stood at the curb in the example above. Were you thinking about other things? Would you have preferred a red light, for instance, to delay your crossing because of a mini-skirted blonde just ahead of you? The point is that the Operations Research solution is not the be-all and end-all. Executive judgment, based upon preconceptions and intuition built on previous experience, must come into play in decision making.

To illustrate the use of a mathematical model in business life, the following case shows the practical use of a mathematical model. The technique used here is called *linear programming*.

A Shipping Problem

We start out with customer orders—a good direction from which to approach almost any business problem. Let us assume that a company manufactures machine tools and has orders for a particular model from the following locations:

Orlando, Florida	3
Tampa, Florida	3
Wichita, Kansas	5
Riverside, California	5
Tucson, Arizona	5
	21

In our example, most of this order can be filled from warehouse stock. We have 17 items on hand of the 21 required. They are located as shown below:

Columbus, Ohio	4
Macon, Georgia	5
Oklahoma City, Oklahoma	8
	17

The problem might be expanded to include the question of where more machine tools should be manufactured, but we will keep it simple by assuming that four of the tools will be manufactured at Columbus, Ohio to balance supply and demand at 21.

The question, then, is: How can we get the 21 items from these locations to the five order points with the fewest possible tonnage miles? This would not seem to be difficult. A likely shipping pattern is shown in Figure 12–1.

The major consideration underlying this pattern seems logical enough: all of Wichita's demand might well be filled from Oklahoma City because of the closeness of those cities. Once this decision is made, the other parts of the pattern are pretty well determined.

We still do not know, however, whether this is really the best shipping pattern or whether tonnage miles might be saved by routing the items by a different plan. Interestingly enough, with the relatively few variables in this problem, there are more than fourteen thousand possible shipping patterns, including a best one and a worst one.

As mentioned earlier, a major aspect of the OR approach is

A likely solution

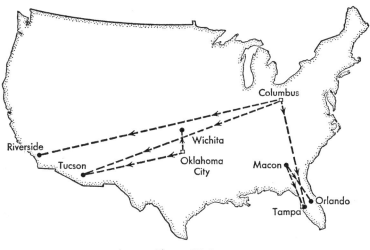

Figure 12–1

the quantification of the elements involved. Table 12–1 combines the customer demand with the supply picture.

TABLE 12–1

Demand		Oklahoma City	Columbus	Macon	Total
		Supply			
		8	8	5	21
Riverside	5				
Tucson	5				
Wichita	5				
Tampa	3				
Orlando	3				
Total	21				

When we add the airline miles between the locations to the customer-demand and supply-picture figures, we have a complete description of the problem as shown in Table 12–2.

TABLE 12–2

Demand		Supply			
		Oklahoma City	Columbus	Macon	Total
		8	8	5	21
Riverside	5	1,030	1,795	1,818	
Tucson	5	824	1,590	1,416	
Wichita	5	136	716	806	
Tampa	3	938	905	346	
Orlando	3	995	854	296	
Total	21				

At this point we have developed all the required data for solving the problem. And we have set down the problem in a way that allows the mathematician to find the lowest tonnage-mile solution. The method of doing this—linear programming—is an Operations Research technique that has been particularly useful to business to date. From the standpoint of business applications, linear programming solves allocation problems. In our example, we want the allocation of supply and demand mated in the most efficient manner.

The most efficient shipping pattern is shown in Figure 12–2 along with the previously shown likely solution.

In an effort to simplify the problem and establish our principle more clearly, the possibility of varying costs of trucking between warehouses has been disregarded.

Our mathematical approach to this problem guarantees us that no better shipping pattern can be found. In this case, of the more than 14,000 possible answers, the worst possible solution would result in 25,480 ton-miles. The likely solution we chose earlier resulted in 17,792 ton-miles, and the best shipping schedule (called the "optimum" in research jargon) would total 16,864 ton-miles. This is an extremely simple problem, but it still results in a great number of possible solutions. As the number of variables increases, the complexity of the problem rises markedly, and application of management judgment without some tool becomes increasingly dif-

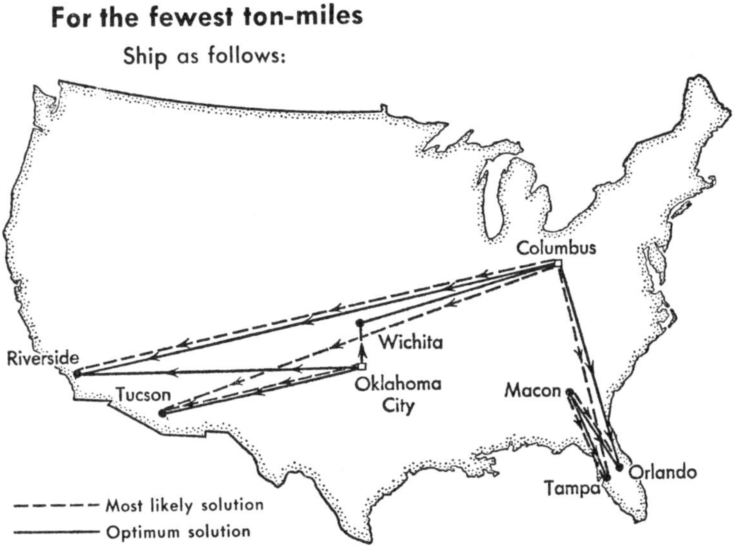

For the fewest ton-miles

Ship as follows:

Figure 12–2

ficult. Because of this fact, Operations Research really gained its greatest impetus only after computers had been developed for working out answers to complex problems.

How Operations Research Can Be Helpful

There are no completely unsolved business problems, but for many problems the solutions can be improved. Through Operations Research, better solutions can be established in the following five basic ways:

1. *Precision.* More accurate statements of relationships (for example, marginal costs vs. average costs) can be obtained.

2. *Depth.* More variables which may affect answers can be considered at the same time. It has been said that most human beings can consider only three variables in their minds at any one time. The use of OR does away with such limitation.

3. *Scope.* An Operations Research statement of a problem and solutions can allow for many more alternatives and contingencies than could be considered otherwise.

4. *Responsiveness.* Once a problem is set up, answers can be arrived at almost instantaneously through the use of a computer.

5. *Cost.* When the method of solving a problem is arrived at, comparable problems can be solved at very low cost.

When and How to Use Operations Research

Before taking even the first step toward the use of Operations Research as a management planning tool, some solid judgment should be applied.

In the first place, one should always ask, "Are we attacking the right problems?" For example, although it may be of great interest to determine how a product may be manufactured most cheaply, the real question might well be whether the product should be manufactured at all. Pinpointing the "right problems" is not easy, but it is an issue that should be thought through carefully before unleashing the forces of Operations Research to find answers.

Second, how important is it to improve the answers we are now getting? If the "pay-off," even assuming that an ideal solution can be obtained, is negligible, then efforts should be bent in a different direction.

Another question to ask is whether appropriate technology for solving a specific problem is available. If techniques have been developed and proven methods can be applied at a known cost in time and money, the decision as to whether to move ahead is relatively clear. If techniques have not yet been developed, the obvious question is whether the development of such techniques is feasible and justifiable economically.

Earlier we mentioned that a major obstacle to broader understanding of Operations Research is the technical nature of the tools the researcher uses. The problem here is the confusion between what one is trying to do—*the problem and the approach*—which is all the businessman needs to know, and *the specific techniques,* mostly mathematical, which are used to do the job.

The highest hurdle to rapid acceptance of Operations Research by business has been the practitioners themselves. The ideal OR man, from a business standpoint, should have the following attributes:

1. He must have education, training, and experience in analytical technique.

2. He must be research-minded *and* operations-oriented.

3. His proposed solutions must be clear, concise, and understandable to the businessman. This, once again, does not mean that the businessman must understand the rationale of every agonizing detail of the calculations, but he must understand both the solution and its implications.

4. He must talk the businessman's language. And, dear reader, to coin a phrase, "they don't hardly make 'em like that no more."

When and how to use Operations Research profitably involves intimate knowledge of one's own business, careful, well-informed judgment as to what the important factors are, and skillful selection of the areas to which Operations Research talents should be applied.

Characteristics of Operations Research

Some characteristics of Operations Research are objectivity, measurement, use of models, and testing of conclusions.

OBJECTIVITY. Operations Research techniques can produce only objective results. In some cases, as will be noted, certain assumptions may be made in setting up OR problems which may necessarily be somewhat subjective. On the other hand, once the OR man gets hold of these assumptions, they become facts for all practical purposes and no further subjectivity enters into the solutions.

MEASUREMENT. Operations Research deals in measurement, either by direct observation of the facts involved or by the development of a range of probable values. Again, it is completely quantitative.

USE OF MODELS. Typically, models are set up that represent the relationships among the factors in the problem and that allow the testing of alternatives. Although other types of models may be used, mathematical methods such as linear programming are fairly common and are used to compare various possible solutions, the best of which points to the course of action to be taken.

TESTING OF CONCLUSIONS. In every case, and as the problem is being solved, various possible conclusions are being tested, one against the other.

Summary

Although Operations Research has been oversold, it can contribute materially to the solution of many business problems. It cannot be used to simulate the operation of a business as a whole, because it relies upon factors which can be quantified and hence expressed mathematically. It can assist a manager in specific areas of his business operation by increasing his judgment through greater precision, depth, scope, and responsiveness, frequently at less cost than he is now paying for facts he needs.

To use OR a mathematical background is not necessary. On the other hand, finding a competent OR man who speaks the businessman's language is not easy.

Operations Research is not a single technique; it is rather a term encompassing a number of scientific approaches to problem solving. Some of these are relatively old techniques; some are fairly new. In the chapters that follow, we will explore the most useful of these techniques. Chapter 13 is an example of a straightforward mathematical approach to a fairly common inventory management problem. Succeeding chapters cover the following techniques:

Accounting for Risk
System Simulation
Queuing Theory

Statistical Inference
Mathematical Programming
Critical Path Scheduling
Summary: Usefulness of Operations Research in Planning and Control

None of these chapters contains any mathematical formulas, not even a summation sign. These are not necessary for the executive's understanding of Operations Research.

13 An Inventory Problem:
A Determinate Solution

Operations Research is basically an approach to problems, one that seeks to quantify all possible variables and put them in relationship to one another. This chapter should give the reader a better feel for this process, showing how a specific company (names have been changed) used Operations Research to help solve an important inventory management problem. We will give some indication of the thinking that an OR approach entails, some of the kinds of questions that might be asked, and a few other considerations involved.

The Company

The Johnson Plumbing Supply Company, Inc., makes and distributes plumbing supplies to wholesalers. Total sales per year are currently about $10,000,000. The company stocks about 1,000 items, of which it fabricates about 400 and buys the other 600 from other manufacturers to fill out the line for marketing purposes. About 80 per cent of sales are of items fabricated in the plant. Johnson is highly respected in the field for both quality and service, but in recent years as it has grown, it has become increasingly affected by price competition.

In the last three years, sales have risen from $7,000,000 to $10,000,000, but profit before taxes on invested capital has decreased from 20 to 16 per cent. A new financial vice-president has been brought into the company, and he has started a product-by-product review to determine how profits can be increased.

The Product

Product X is used in the assembly of one of Johnson's major product lines. In normal use, it tends to wear out before the rest of the product; for this reason, there is fairly steady demand for it. Product X is essential to the operation of the assembly, and when it is needed, service is important. Competitive companies make the equivalent of Product X, but Johnson prides itself on service and feels its image would suffer if its distributors could not supply Johnson-brand Product X.

Despite the replacement market, demand for Product X has not grown in recent years, and holds steady at about 12,000 units, fairly evenly spread over the year.

Johnson's production manager takes great pride in his low cost operation. He says there is not a plant in the country which can come close to his unit costs on every product he makes. His products are also of consistently high quality.

Johnson's marketing manager feels that the service he gives his customers is the real secret of the company's success. He makes certain that no product is ever out of stock and has trained his people to react instantly to distributor demands.

The Scene: An Operating Committee Meeting

Financial Vice-President: "Based upon my previous experience, it appears evident that we have too heavy an investment in inventories. The company raised $1,000,000 in additional capital two years ago, but percentage return on capital has declined and is continuing to decline while sales are rising. This doesn't make financial sense to me.

"In studying the reasons for our achieving lower return on investment than we should, I have analyzed our inventory policy on some of our products. Take Product X, for example, one of our time-honored money-makers. Demand is fairly consistent throughout the year at 1,000 per month. We manufacture a year's supply—12,000 —over a four-week period at the beginning of the year. A new manufacturing order is triggered when inventory reaches 1,200, so that typically we make this part only once a year. Standard cost of this item is $20. Hence, on the average we have 6 months' supply on hand at a cost of $120,000. I'm saying to you that we can use that $120,000 in more productive ways and this inventory should therefore be cut, and cut sharply."

Sales Vice-President: "You're new here and probably don't understand. Johnson Plumbing has built its entire existence on service to the customer. We cannot afford to ever be out of stock. I'm for whatever level of inventories we need to be able to serve our customers."

Financial Vice-President: "Okay, okay. I'm not arguing with you on that point. But how in the hell can you tell me that you need an average of 6,000 items in stock to satisfy a demand of 1,000 a month? It seems to me you could make 1,000 items every month and be assured of service to customers and at the same time cut way back on your inventory carrying costs."

Production Vice President: "Now wait a minute. You talk about wanting to save money; yet you want to increase the annual number of orders on Product X from one to twelve. I know a little about saving money, and that's not the way. Every time we schedule an order, the paper work is tremendous. I'm understaffed now in production scheduling. You've got to understand that I can't just say to my machines 'Get ready to make Product X.' To prepare to make Product X, I've got to count on 20 hours of setup time. This is time spent by the best mechanics we have—with overhead you're talking about $200 for setup alone. Also, our operators have to get used to production of Product X. Spoilage is always tremendous the first day of production. And you're talking about saving money!"

President: "It seems as if everybody has a different point of view here. Let's look at this problem logically, see how we can increase profits, and still satisfy everybody."

Is There a Solution?

To the experienced businessman, the above dialogue must sound familiar. Each of the protagonists, in effect, has his own model, his sets of goals, his way of achieving them. Typically, the president would step in and arrive at a solution which would improve the situation but might well not be the best solution possible because even his analysis might have but limited precision, depth, and scope. This is where Operation Research comes in. In effect, a much better model is needed.

There are no set, programmed steps to follow in trying to develop a better model. Nor is there any test to prove that a given model is the best possbile. Construction of the model, in this as in many OR situations, requires knowledge of business, insight, and under-standing of the relationships involved.

The businessman himself knows better than anyone else what makes his business tick. It is his responsibility to guide the opera-tions researcher as to what is important. At the same time, the businessman must keep an open mind as to things he has not thought about, which may be important.

Focusing on our present problem, let's summarize the preceding discussion.

1. Because of the importance of maintaining service, Johnson never wants to be out of stock.

2. By manufacturing Product X only once a year, substantial production cost savings can be achieved.

Whether these two factors should be considered as guides in making policy is in serious doubt. If these factors are accepted as the only ones of importance, it might make sense to manufacture Product X only every 5 years, or even every 10 years, when even higher production savings can be achieved. Think of the inventory carrying costs here!

The real answer, of course, is to look at these factors in their total environment. Some of the unanswered questions are: What are the costs of carrying inventories? Is there a possibility of obsolescence? How serious is an out-of-stock problem once in one hundred times, or once in one thousand? Are there better alternative uses for the capital needed to carry inventories? Are price rises in labor and/or materials anticipated and in what degree? Obviously, many other logical questions could be raised.

To simplify the present situation, we shall assume:

1. Being out of stock is to be avoided at all costs.
2. Demand will remain steady at 1,000 per month.
3. A 20 per cent return on capital, pre-tax, can be obtained in other fields.
4. Obsolescence can be determined a year or more ahead of time.
5. Increases in wages and material costs can be recouped immediately through price increases (possibly not a realistic assumption, but please bear with us).

Thus we come down to the basic problem of what it costs us to make and carry inventories. The further questions that must then be answered are these:

1. What are clerical costs of placing an order?
2. What are purchasing costs for raw materials, including quantity discounts?
3. What are setup costs, including spoilage at beginning of run?
4. What are trucking costs from factory to warehouse?
5. What are storage costs—rent, clerical, heat, taxes, etc.?
6. What is the cost of capital invested?
7. What spoilage is involved in handling product?
8. How much capital is invested?

Quantification

Finding numerical values for the various factors bearing on the solution of a problem can be a chore. The type of cost information needed is not generally shown in accounting statements.

For example, at Johnson Plumbing it was obvious that a decision affecting the number of orders placed during the year should take into account the clerical costs of placing an order. Moreover, standard costs on items included an overhead allocation factor, presumably to cover order-placing clerical costs, among others. But nobody knew how costs would actually change if the number of manufacturing orders were changed.

Also, defining costs which are relevant to the solution of the problem may not be easy. If Johnson had a long-term lease on a warehouse and were unable to sublet any portion of the space available, a decline in inventories might not produce savings in warehouse costs for some time to come.

The real question to be asked is, "What costs will change as the result of the decisions made?"

In analyzing this problem, after a good amount of both detailed grubbing and considered judgment, the Johnson management decided that the most important costs that varied with number of production orders and inventory sizes were:

Setup, per order	$200
Clerical costs, per order	20
Start-up spoilage and lost efficiency, per order	100
Total important fixed costs per order	$320

At the same time, detailed study revealed that carrying cost per unit of Product X averaged about $2 per year. Management recognized that these figures were not exact, but felt that they were probably within 5 to 10 per cent of being so.

Now management was ready to see if a change in ordering and

manufacturing policy would produce results significant to the operation.

Table 13–1 shows how these admittedly rough estimates were put into an arithmetic model:

TABLE 13–1

No. of Units Per Order	No. of Orders Per Year	Average Inventory	Per Order Costs	Carrying Costs	Total Costs
12,000	1	6,000	$ 320	$12,000	$12,320
6,000	2	3,000	640	6,000	6,640
4,000	3	2,000	960	4,000	4,960
3,000	4	1,500	1,280	3,000	4,280
2,000	6	1,000	1,920	2,000	3,920
1,000	12	500	3,840	1,000	4,840

Converting tables of numbers into graphs can be helpful to persons who are not "numbers-oriented." Figure 13–1 demonstrates how cost benefits on both sides (costs of carrying inventories versus costs of frequent manufacture) trade off one against the other and the point at which minimum total costs can be reached.

This rough solution indicates potential savings in excess of $8,000 per year by changing policies on manufacturing and inventorying Product X alone. If Product X is typical, a reevaluation of policies on all other manufactured items might well result in savings of over $500,000 per year. This possibility stimulated the Johnson management to consider a much more all-inclusive, considerably more complicated analysis of all manufacturing and inventorying policies.

Policy could have been changed on this one item, Product X, from 1-time-a-year ordering to 6 times a year, and at the same time have caused hardly a ripple in the plant's over-all operations. But, if this is just one of many available potential cost savings, the effects of such policy changes could be substantial. Some of the new questions that might be raised for Johnson are: Can we hire more competent setup men or must we train them? Is new machinery necessary and

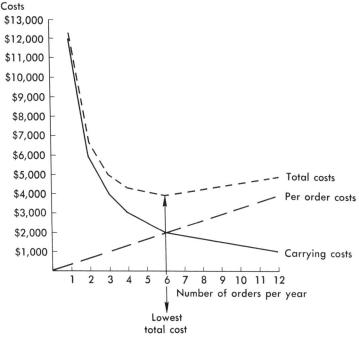

Figure 13–1. Product X—Relevant Costs per Order

how soon would it pay for itself? Do we want to expand the plant or go into shift operations? How can we develop scheduling capacity that might be needed? Should we be thinking in terms of buying or leasing a computer? How long would it take and what would the cost be to develop a more sophisticated, faster ordering system?

Summary

We have indicated a simple Operations Research approach to a concrete business problem. At the same time we have tried to suggest that the deeper one goes into a problem, the more complex it becomes, and the greater the need for competent managerial talent to quantify what is quantifiable and, at the same time, to weigh qualitative factors and keep them in proper perspective for good decision making.

14 Handling the Risk Factor

Most major decisions that businessmen make involve a decided element of risk. In the preceding chapter, for example, we assumed that the Johnson Company could count on continuing level demand for Product X. In real life this kind of situation rarely occurs. In the case of the Johnson Company we assumed that all conditions surrounding the problem were known. This allowed us to create what is known in the jargon of the trade as a deterministic model.

Typically, there are many uncertainties when one tries to look into the future, even when the record of the past is completely clear. We generally have too little knowledge of cause and effect, and, even when we do know causes, we find them too complex to measure.

Where uncertainties exist (and this is most of the time), OR can be of assistance in equating the magnitude of the risks involved with the chance of success, so that the businessman can make a better-informed decision.

A Simple Problem

Max, the fruit vendor, at the corner of Broadway and Fulton Street in New York, faces a purchasing decision every day which provides an illustration of decision making under uncertainty. (Although the amounts of money involved here may not seem important to the reader, they are to Max; so no condescension is in order.)

Max buys fruit every morning to sell at his stand. During the season he sells fresh peaches. He buys peaches at $8 per case and sells them at a retail price that brings him $10 per case. Admittedly, this is a low mark-up, but the business is competitive and this is the best price he can get. Any cases he cannot sell, he unloads to a canner's agent at night for $2 a case.

Max never knows at the beginning of the day how many cases he will be able to sell, although his experience has been that on some days he will not sell even 1 case but on some lucky days he may sell as many as 4 cases. (We are assuming for convenience that he deals in full cases only.)

A look at the weather each morning is some help, but Max still has a tough decision to make every day: how many cases should he buy?

If he buys 4 cases and can sell only 1, for example, he loses $16, as follows:

Cost of peaches (4 @ $8)		$32
Sales:		
To public (1 @ $10)	$10	
To canner (3 @ $2)	6	16
Net loss		($16)

To help him make up his mind as to what he might gain or lose, Max constructs an arithmetic model called a pay-off table (Table 14-1), which gives him at a glance the net result of his buying strategy at varying levels of demand.

Now Max has a clear-cut quantified choice to make. The criterion he should use is obvious—he should choose the most profitable

TABLE 14–1

Buying Strategy (Number of Cases)	Demand (Number of Cases)				
	0	1	2	3	4
0	$ 0	$ 0	$ 0	$0	$0
1	(6)*	2	2	2	2
2	(12)	(4)	4	4	4
3	(18)	(10)	(2)	6	6
4	(24)	(16)	(8)	0	8

* Figures in parentheses indicate losses.

strategy. But under risk conditions, the answer is not readily apparent, because it is not obvious which strategy is the most profitable. Max is going to make his decision based upon the kind of guy he is, and it is likely he will make one of three choices, which we have put in OR terms:

1. CRITERION OF PESSIMISM. This assumes that nature is out to get you; that no matter what you do, the worst possible result will occur. Hence, you choose the strategy that will lose you the least, if everything goes bad (see Table 14–2).

TABLE 14–2

If Max Chooses This Strategy	The Worst Result Is	And the Pay-off Is
Buy 0	Demand 0	$ 0
1	0	(6)
2	0	(12)
3	0	(18)
4	0	(24)

Using this criteron, the best decision is not to buy peaches.

2. CRITERION OF OPTIMISM. This, the opposite of criterion 1, assumes that luck is with you, that no matter what you do, everything will turn out well. Hence, you choose the strategy that will make the most money for you under the most favorable conditions (see Table 14–3).

TABLE 14–3

If Max Chooses This Strategy	The Best Result Is	And the Pay-off Is
Buy 0	Demand 0	$0
1	1	2
2	2	4
3	3	6
4	4	8

Using this criterion, the best decision is to buy 4 cases.

3. CRITERION OF LEAST REGRET. If Max chooses a certain buying strategy and this strategy turns out to be the best one he could have chosen, based upon sales, he will feel no regret. On the other hand, based on sales, if he feels he should have chosen a different strategy, he will feel regret; and the difference between his actual pay-off and what he might have made had he bought differently is a good measure of his regret. He now gropes for some numbers to measure his potential regret. (See Table 14–4).

TABLE 14–4

If I Have Bought	Regret for Demands of				
	0	1	2	3	4
0	$ 0	$ 2	$ 4	$6	$8
1	6	0	2	4	6
2	12	6	0	2	4
3	18	12	6	0	2
4	24	18	12	6	0

From this model we can see that, if he buys no cases of peaches, he could lose a potential profit of $8, if he had a market for 4 cases. To sum up, his greatest regret based upon various buying levels would be as shown in Table 14–5.

If Max follows the criterion of least regret, his best bet is to buy 1 case each day.

Although these criteria are used in solving some risk-taking problems, they are really pretty naive if used without managerial

TABLE 14–5

If He Bought	The Most He Could Lose Is
0	$ 8
1	6
2	12
3	18
4	24

judgment. The first criterion would suggest going out of business. The second advocates becoming a plunger, even if the odds are substantially against you. The third, a better approach, is still badly focused in that it concentrates on losing the least possible instead of maximizing your profits.

Businessmen who use any of these approaches as the sole basis for decision making are fooling themselves if they claim to be taking a calculated risk. Taking a calculated risk means balancing risks against profit opportunities, then adopting the strategy that has the most profitable level of risk. Decision making under conditions of uncertainty requires some means of quantifying the inherent risks in different strategies. We must be able to measure risk and compare it to the profit opportunity that risk implies.

Probability as a Yardstick

The concept of "probability" provides us with a means of quantifying risk. We have gone to some length to show the problems of making decisions under conditions of uncertainty and that we need some method to measure risk. Probability is a way of measuring this risk.

Cutting through the academic verbiage that usually accompanies the concept of probability, what we mean by the probability of an event occurring is simply the likelihood (or our degree of belief) that the event will take place. To use the old coin-flipping example, we say that the probability of a head on the flip of a coin is 50 per cent (or .5 in decimal notation). By saying this, we mean that we expect that in a large number of flips, heads will show up 50 per cent of the time.

Now let us go back to Max with the probability concept. He has been selling peaches for a long time and may even have some records of what number he has sold in the past. We recognize that weather conditions, religious holidays, and other factors may cause marked changes from normal, but let's ask him what probabilities he would attach to the eventuality of demand for 0, 1, 2, 3, or 4 cases on a normal day.

He tells us that, based on his experience, the probability of sales at different levels is as follows:

TABLE 14–6

Demand	Probability	Cumulative
0	5%	5%
1	15	20
2	25	45
3	35	80
4	20	100

At this point we can incorporate these probabilities into his original pay-off table and come up with Table 14–7.

TABLE 14–7

	Demand (Number of Cases)				
	0	1	2	3	4
Probability of this demand	.05	.15	.25	.35	.20
Probability of this demand or less	.05	.20	.45	.80	1.00
Strategy to buy					
0 cases	$ 0	$ 0	$ 0	$0	$0
1 case	(6)	2	2	2	2
2 cases	(12)	(4)	4	4	4
3 cases	(18)	(10)	(6)	6	6
4 cases	(24)	(16)	(8)	0	8

Although this table has been logically constructed, a good businessman will have no idea how to use it to his own advantage. So we explain to Max that the table allows us now to compare the different risk/profit opportunities of his various buying strategies. Incorporating probabilities into our mathematical model allows us to say:

> If we buy no peaches, we will lose nothing.
> If we buy 1 case, we have a 5 per cent chance of being worse off by $6 in exchange for a 95 per cent chance of being better off by $2.
> To go to the far end of the spectrum, we can tell Max that if he buys 4 cases instead of 1, he has a 20 per cent chance of selling all 4 cases, hence making $6 more than if he bought 1.
> But he has an 80 per cent chance that he will be at least $2 worse off than if he had bought only 1 case, and there is a 20 per cent chance that he would be $18 worse off.

These statements should be of help to the businessman. We have not established criteria to accept or reject any of the possible strategies, but we have given him data so that he can make a judgment as to which combination of risk/profit best suits his situation. He now has a fairly clear-cut, logical procedure for comparing different risk and profit opportunities.

Expected Values

We hope that, at this point, we have established the usefulness of probability as a measure of risk. This concept can be exceedingly helpful to management in trying to decide among the relative desirabilities of different strategies under conditions of uncertainty. There is no magic in this, however. Every businessman has to assess the risk versus the potential return and decide what his course of action should be.

In this regard, the businessman must always have in mind the selection of the strategy with the highest expected profit. And this highest expected profit is the profit which he expects to earn *on the average* by adopting the strategy.

We determine the expected profit of a strategy by multiplying the profit of each of the possible outcomes by the probability of their occurrence, and then adding the results. Really all we are doing is taking a weighted average of each of the possible outcomes.

Now back to poor old Max. Table 14–8 shows the situation if he buys 3 cases.

TABLE 14–8

Demand Could Be	Giving a Profit of	The Probability of This Is	Profit × Probability
0	$(18)	.05	(.90)
1	(10)	.15	(1.50)
2	(2)	.25	(.50)
3	6	.35	2.10
4	6	.20	1.20
Expected profit over-all			$0.40

The logic behind this calculation is relatively simple. We are using the law of probability (harking back to the expectation that a coin flipped many times will come up heads 50 per cent of the time). We are now saying that over many normal days (say 100, for this example), since 0 demand will occur 5 per cent of the time, there will be:

5 days on which demand would be 0
15 days on which demand would be 1
25 days on which demand would be 2
35 days on which demand would be 3
20 days on which demand would be 4

Table 14–9 restates Table 14–8 in a different and perhaps more understandable form, still for the situation where Max buys 3 cases each day.

The answer, less than coincidentally, shows that Max's profit for 100 days is $40.00, or 100 days of the $.40 per day profit shown in Table 14–8.

In constructing this example, however, we assumed, for no particular reason, the purchase of 3 cases of peaches a day, with no knowledge of alternative results. Using the same probabilities, the

TABLE 14–9

Demand Would Be	On Days	Profit Earned on Each Day	Probable Gain or (Loss)
0	5	$(18)	$ (90)
1	15	(10)	(150)
2	25	(2)	(50)
3	35	6	210
4	20	6	120
Total profit for 100 days			$ 40

reader can relatively quickly compute the expected average per day profits at other levels for purchasing peaches with the results shown in Table 14–10.

TABLE 14–10

Buy Cases	Expected Profit
0	0
1	$ 1.60
2	2.00
3	.40
4	(3.55)

It should be emphasized that the expected profit of a strategy does not tell you how much you are likely to earn on any given day by adopting that strategy. The answer must be the average profit experience you would expect to have over a long period of time. To cite a proverb, "What you lose on the peaches, you make up on the bananas."

At the same time, it is valid to use the expected value criterion on a one-shot operation. For example, if Max were retiring tomorrow, it would be completely valid for him to use the criteria set forth above in deciding what to do today. He might well lose; a different strategy on this particular day might make him more money; but the odds are with him to follow the strategy of buying 2 cases of peaches a day.

Before leaving this subject, we should point out that, despite thorough consideration of the odds, there are constraints which may lead to managerial decisions other than those based upon expected value.

It is conceivable that at a certain time in his career, Max could not afford to lose $12 on a given day. If this were true, he would have to take a less risky strategy than that of buying 2 cases of peaches, even though his less risky strategy would have a lower expected profit.

Generally, if the sums of money that the decision involves are small relative to the total asset position of the decision maker, highest expected value is the most rational criterion. For instance, the well-to-do person who goes to the race track occasionally for fun might well be expected to bet on long shots rather than playing the favorites to show.

In any business situation, however, the manager should always insist on knowing the range of possible results as well as the expected values.

Sources of Probability Measurements

The reader should now be ready to agree that probabilities as a measure of risk are useful, but he may raise the pertinent question, "How do I determine the probability of specific events happening at certain future times?"

The most frequently used source of probability data is past history. Statistical analysis of historical data, which can indicate what has happened when and under what influences in the past, can be extremely helpful. (More will be said on this subject in Chapter 17.)

But we may not have historical data available, or even if we have it, it may not always be relevant; changes may well have occurred that have made it obvious that future conditions will not be related to historical experience.

When this situation prevails, we must fall back on subjective estimation, which merely means educated guessing. Many academicians refuse to recognize the validity of the educated guess, saying that there must be a better way. Those with this view must take substantial responsibility for the communications gap between OR practitioners and businessmen.

How good subjective probabilities actually are can be (and has been) discussed far into the night without much light being shed on the answer. Of course there is a good chance that the probabilities will be inaccurate. The only thing that is relatively certain is that the educated guess is about as good as the judgment of the businessman making it. But do not scoff at the good businessman's intuition. Although intuitive decisions may appear to be made without rational thought, it is my experience that the good businessman's judgment really reflects instantaneous recall of like situations and results drawn from his background and experience. Even if he cannot articulate his reasoning, his subjective probabilities frequently come from the finest computer of them all—the human brain.

Summary

Whether formalized or not, many business decisions are made based upon the businessman's opinion of the probability of success of the venture. If both the potential pay-off of alternative decisions and the probable success of each can be quantified, the decision-making process can be considerably simplified. Even when complete quantification cannot be approximated, the rigor of attempting to quantify, even by the use of educated guesses, can be of great help in producing the best answer.

15   System Simulation

System simulation is probably the most frequently used technique in Operations Research. Basically, it is used to determine the answer to the question, "What would happen if . . .?"; it is really an extension of trial-and-error experimentation.

One of the ablest OR practitioners I know contends that simulation is useful only when you do not understand the problem you are trying to solve. However, when pressed, he admits that at some point he uses simulation in connection with nearly all of the OR problems on which he works. This is because the problem, as described to him by a business manager, may not be the real problem at all, and simulation may be a good way to find out what the real problem is.

To explain the development and application of simulation from the origin of its need up to the present day, we shall use two examples, emphasizing practical uses rather than technical development.

Trial-and-Error Solution: The Axe

Certainly not all problems need to be solved by use of a simulation technique. Take, for example, the axe, a device that solves many problems and that was developed by our primitive ancestors with such success that we have not significantly improved on it in thousands of years, except in materials and methods of manufacture. To the best of our knowledge, the Stone Age axe was developed by pure trial-and-error experimentation. Improvements came as a result of making axes according to varying ideas and trying them out. It is highly improbable that models, mechanical analysis, or any other forms of simulation were employed.

Thus, problems *can* be solved by simple trial and error. But remember that certain conditions contributed markedly to the success of this method.

FEW VARIABLES. The relatively small number of variables (for example, weight and shape of head, length of handle, and strength) involved in an axe limits the number of possible combinations, so that a reasonable number of trials is sufficient to explore all worthwhile possibilities.

CHEAP MISTAKES. It doesn't cost very much to make an axe.

PLENTY OF TIME. Based on what archaeology tells us, it appears that our Stone Age ancestors had no great conscious need to improve their methods overnight.

We can say, then, that this example and others similar provide historical evidence that pure trial-and-error experimentation is a successful method of solving problems where mistakes are not costly and time is not important. Historical evidence, however, shows that other problems have not yielded so readily to the trial-and-error approach.

Evolution of Simulation: Bridge Design

Looking at history again, it appears pretty clear that the first bridges were created as a result of natural happenstance—a tree falling across a river. Certainly the idea of making such a bridge by laying tree trunks across a river would naturally follow. This level of bridge building was reached among many early peoples, but was not found during the days of the Roman Empire. The

Romans needed bridges that could support numerous troops at one time; and according to historical accounts, they had many failures.

As a matter of fact, the Romans never solved the bridge *design* problem, but they did learn how to *construct* bridges. By using five or ten times the amount of masonry and labor needed, they built bridges that were usable and that withstood heavy loads. Sheer massiveness of construction—extravagance, we might call it—made these bridges serviceable, rather than efficiency of design. Since labor was valued at a very low rate, these designs were not really uneconomic by the standards of the time.

In the seventeenth and eighteenth centuries, however, rising labor costs and financing problems created pressures to conserve labor and material resources. Attempts to lighten bridges were begun, again through trial and error. Failures were frequent and progress was slow, because the testing time for each new idea was equal to the time it took to build a bridge plus some reasonable period of use. A new need arose: the ability to carry out the equivalent of trial-and-error experiments in some way that would be quicker and cheaper than the building of full-scale structures.

Enter the first models. Today it is commonplace to use scale-model simulation for aircraft, ship, and industrial plant design. But in 1732, when the French engineer, Denisy, used a scale-model simulation technique to study the failures of masonry arches, it was a major scientific step forward. Of particular interest is the fact that he did not model whole bridges because it was evident to him that the heart of the bridge problem was the need for a strong, lightweight arch. (We say this is of particular interest because one of the major mistakes made by businessmen in using simulation techniques is that of trying to model an entire problem with many variables rather than zeroing in on the important factors.)

Meanwhile M. Denisy had pointed the way to an improved bridge design, which was soon reflected in new bridges all over France. As years went by, it was found that bridge structures could be simulated by mathematical techniques even more quickly and cheaply, with stresses and strains forecast mathematically. Eventually, simulation reached the point where a suspension bridge could be designed and built entirely without trial-and-error technique.

The Principles of Simulation

These rather homely examples have been cited in an attempt to show how the simulation technique, now widely used in business, has evolved. We have seen how increasingly complex problems and pressures for more efficient use of time, labor, and material resources almost demanded the development of substitutes for full-scale, trial-and-error experimentation. We also might note two practical observations which apply to all applications of the simulation technique.

1. *An efficient simulation represents only significant details of the full-scale system.* Although those who build full-scale models as a hobby pride themselves on exquisite rendering of detail, effective simulation models are actually pared to the minimum of detail and only the essentials are considered (for example, Denisy's arches).

2. *A management decision must be made to determine what factors are important.* If a bridge designer were to neglect to consider the effect of prevailing winds, for example, his intricate calculations of load factors, stresses, and so forth, might well result in an inadequate structure.

We have established that simulation is really the use of the trial-and-error technique, but on paper. System simulation is the attempt to set down on paper the real world and to experiment with it. By this we mean we first set up a model—a mathematical representation of the system—and by tinkering with the model we try to find out what are the major variables that cause the system to work the way it does. Then, by working through the mathematics of the model, we imitate on paper the actual workings of the system. If a computer is available, we can simulate in minutes on paper what might take years of actual activity. We can propose successive changes to the system and test them in relationship to other fixed and variable factors. If through our experimentation on paper we are satisfied with specific proposed changes, we can now take them into the business world and have a pretty good idea how they will work.

It may be useful to go through an illustration of a fairly simple use of the simulation process in a business setting.

A Business Systems Simulation Problem

Let us assume we operate a factory which is almost fully automated. A key element in the plant's operation is a relatively inexpensive but very important unit called an XKE. There are three of these units in the plant.

XKEs have an unusual life cycle. Only 50 per cent of them operate efficiently for as long as 30 days, but those that do not break down in the first 30 days are normally good for 3 more months.

Whenever an XKE breaks down, we have to call an authorized repairman to replace it. The normal charge for service is $100 per call plus $10 for every unit replaced. (To avoid complications of factory downtime, etc., in this problem, we are assuming instantaneous reaction and service.)

We have been following the policy of replacing units as they break down but have recently begun to wonder whether this is the most economic policy. Specifically, we wonder if it might not be cheaper to replace *all* units whenever one breaks down. On the surface, this would appear to save us money because the serviceman's per call rate is so high relative to the cost of the part itself.

In this case we can simulate two alternate decisions: (1) replace each unit when it breaks down, or (2) replace all units if any one breaks down.

We are assuming that each unit breaks down at the end of a month or at the end of 4 months, only to make the example easier to follow. Obviously, had we kept historical records, the exact time of breakdowns could have been used in the model. Since we have assumed that each unit will have a life of 1 month or 4 months and that 50 per cent of the units break down at each of these two intervals, we can by a head-or-tails sampling arrangement arrive at what breakdowns may be expected when.

If we assume that we will replace only the bad unit at the time of each breakdown, Table 15–1 shows the way things would have operated over a two-year period:

Assuming that all breakdowns occur at month-end, the above experience table shows that the serviceman made 17 calls to replace

TABLE 15–1

Month	Unit Number		
	1	2	3
1	5*	5	2
2	—	—	6
3	—	—	—
4	—	—	—
5	6	6	—
6	7	10	10
7	11	—	—
8	—	—	—
9	—	—	—
10	—	14	14
11	12	—	—
12	13	—	—
13	14	—	—
14	15	15	18
15	19	19	—
16	—	—	—
17	—	—	—
18	—	—	22
19	23	20	—
20	—	24	—
21	—	—	—
22	—	—	26
23	27	—	—
24	—	28	—

* Number in Unit column indicates replacement month.

27 units. Total cost at $100 per call plus $10 per unit replaced was $1,970.

Changing our decision to replace all units if one breaks down, the month-by-month simulation works out as shown in Table 15–2.

Under this decision the simulated two-year experience results in 13 service calls and 39 replacements for a total cost of $1,690.

Before jumping to any conclusions about the relative efficiency of these two decisions, it would be desirable to extend the simulation for well over two years. Ten or fifteen years might lend much more valid results, and on a computer such an extension could be

TABLE 15–2

	Unit Number		
Month	1	2	3
1	5*	5	2
2	6	3	3
3	4	7	7
4	8	8	8
5	—	—	—
6	—	—	—
7	—	—	—
8	9	9	9
9	10	10	13
10	14	14	14
11	—	—	—
12	—	—	—
13	—	—	—
14	18	15	18
15	19	19	19
16	—	—	—
17	—	—	—
18	—	—	—
19	20	23	23
20	24	21	24
21	25	22	22
22	26	26	26
23	—	—	—
24	—	—	—

* Number in Unit column indicates month that breakdown would have occurred.

handled very quickly. But if the conclusions are to show the same order of attractiveness, it would certainly make sense to consider changing replacement practices.

Summary

System simulation hardly ever leads to an optimum—best—solution. Through simulation you can determine whether one solution is better than another, but even the better solution may not be nearly as good as some other. For example, in our simple example we did not even test the possibility of replacing all units with more than 2 months (or 3 months) of service if one breaks down. One of these policies might yield better results than those we have followed.

Simulation, however, is very useful in handling complex problems where there may be many important variables. Where you know all the facts and the important variables are clear, other mathematical tools such as linear programming may be much more helpful because, based on the given facts, they can arrive at an optimum solution. When the situation is so complex that it is difficult to know how the different variables will affect each other, simulation helps us to understand the problem and to be in a better position to deal with it.

16   Queuing Theory

All of us have suffered the exasperation of waiting in line for something: at the supermarket, waiting to check out purchases; in airplanes, waiting for clearance to land; in the doctor's office, waiting at 3:00 P.M. for a 2:00 P.M. appointment; at toll booths, waiting while the lady ahead digs frantically through her change purse; at the coffee machine; and at the bank, particularly on a Friday noon. While waiting in line in one of these situations, you tend to think, "There must be a better way." This is what Queuing Theory is all about.

Queuing Theory got its start in the first part of this century when telephone engineers, working on the introduction of direct dialing, ran head on into the problem of what kind of equipment and how many lines were needed in order to provide efficient service to their subscribers. This was a sizable problem: at certain times there was negligible demand for phone service, and at other times calls flooded the circuits to the point where they were almost paralyzed.

It was not until after World War II, however, that businessmen really became aware of the many similarities between a telephone company's problem and many industrial situations. Since then it has become well recognized that the "waiting line" is fairly common, and a sophisticated bag of tools has been developed to deal with this problem.

Most businessmen run into waiting-line problems from time to time. The importance of these problems should determine the amount of sophisticated techniques and time to be used in solving them. Queuing Theory has been applied in such complex situations as the design of the most efficient port facilities and in such simple operations as the determination of how many tool bins to have in a shop.

The Model

Schematically, the typical waiting-line problem can be set forth as shown in Figure 16–1.

| Customers | Arrival Rate → | o o o o o
 Waiting Line | Queue → Discipline | Service Capacity
 Service Rate | Serviced → Customers |

Figure 16–1

Very simply, something that needs service, called *customers,* arrives at some rate, called the *Arrival Rate.* If the customers cannot be serviced immediately, they wait in a *Waiting Line.* The *Service Capacity* processes the customers at some rate, called the *Service Rate,* gradually depleting the waiting line (provided that the service rate is greater than the arrival rate). One other term is important—*Queue Discipline*—which defines the rule by which customers in the waiting line are chosen to enter the service capacity (this is usually first-come, first-served, but by no means always).

Table 16–1 gives a few examples of queuing situations.

It should be obvious that the universal question in waiting-line problems is "how large should service capacity be?" Theoretically, in any situation, service capacity could be arranged so that, at any time, immediate service is available.

TABLE 16–1

Customers	Waiting Line	Service Capacity
Ships	Waiting outside port	To dock and unload
Invoices	Sitting on a clerk's desk	To be paid
Airplanes	Stacked in air, waiting	To land
Pedestrians	Waiting on the street	For a taxi
Taxis	Waiting in line	For a fare

The Decision

The basic question in waiting-line problems is economic. On one side, there is the possibility of loss (in most cases, loss of future business through loss of customer good will) if customers are kept waiting too long. On the other side, unused capacity in the service facility can be extremely costly, from the standpoint both of capital investment and day-to-day operating costs.

To arrive at any valid conclusion, one must consider the rate at which customers are likely to arrive (see probabilities discussed in Chapter 7), how long customers are going to be willing to wait, and the costs (both capital and day-to-day) of providing service facilities. Only by balancing these three factors can any rational decision be made.

The Problem

The problem of arrival rates, and how to forecast them, is a significant part of waiting-line situations. Obviously, if an arrival rate is constant, the solution is greatly simplified. If the arrival rate is greater than the service rate, a queue will develop. The greater this difference, the faster the queue will form. If arrival rate and service rate are the same, there will be no waiting line and the service facility will have no idle time. If the service rate is greater than the arrival rate, there will be no waiting line, but there will be idle capacity. Table 16–2 illustrates this point.

Obviously, the best of all worlds exists under the second situation above. Everything is in balance—perfect service and no idle

TABLE 16–2

THE EFFECT ON QUEUE AND IDLE CAPACITY OF A CHANGE
IN THE ARRIVAL RATE (ASSUMING CONSTANT RATES)

End of Minute	Arrival Rate (2 per Minute) Greater than Service Rate (1 per Minute)		Arrival Rate (1 per Minute) Equal to Service Rate (1 per Minute)		Arrival Rate (1 per Minute) Less than Service Rate (2 per Minute)	
	No. in Line	Idle Capacity	No. in Line	Idle Capacity	No. in Line	Idle Capacity
1	1	0	0	0	0	½
2	2	0	0	0	0	1
3	3	0	0	0	0	1½
4	4	0	0	0	0	2
5	5	0	0	0	0	2½
6	6	0	0	0	0	3

capacity. And if we could assume constant rates of arrival, the adjustments to be made under the first and third situations to improve the performance could be easily arrived at. But in real life this kind of situation rarely exists.

Chance Variation

Far more commonly, in any waiting-line situation there are considerable variations both in arrival rates and in the time it takes to service an arrival.

Let us assume, for example, that arrivals vary as follows:

33⅓ % of the time — 1 arrival per minute
33⅓ % of the time — 2 arrivals per minute
33⅓ % of the time — 3 arrivals per minute

and that service rates vary as follows:

25% of the time — 1 arrival serviced per minute
50% of the time — 2 arrivals serviced per minute
25% of the time — 3 arrivals serviced per minute

An obvious question, given the above assumptions, is, In a normal 8-to-5 working day, what will be the average waiting line?

A quick thinker will realize that, on the average, arrivals occur at the rate of 2 per minute, and, on the average, servicing handles 2 arrivals per minute. Hence, the average waiting time is zero—no waiting line and no idle service capacity.

With a little more thought, though, one must realize that this quick, seemingly logical conclusion just is not true. Under the above assumptions, the waiting line will, in fact, grow longer and longer and longer as the day goes on. This is so because experience has proved that an above-average arrival rate will not always be compensated for at the same time by an above-average service rate. When this happens, a line forms which cannot be worked off rapidly. Further, any idle time on the part of a single service facility cannot be put in the bank to be called on later; it simply disappears. A further addition to our waiting lines is caused by variations between lines both in rate of arrival and time taken to service. At any rate, take it from one who has suffered considerable delays by picking the wrong checkout counter at a supermarket, matching *average* rates of arrival and *average* service time does not overcome the waiting-line problem.

Method of Solution

Complex mathematical tools have been developed to accommodate the difficulties that result from variations in arrival and service rates. Queuing Theory models can give answers to such questions as the following:

How long will the average customer have to wait?

What is the longest time any customer will have to wait?

How long will the longest waiting line be?

How much idle capacity will there be?

What effect will a given change in service capacity have on the above questions?

Most Queuing Theory problems are solved through the use of simulation techniques, which you will remember from Chapter 15 are variations on the question "What would happen if . . . ?" Simulation is especially useful in solving this type of problem because there is generally high capital cost involved in increasing service capacity, and the businessman wants to find out what the results are likely to be before he spends sizable sums for capital improvements. Also, the relationships between interacting variables (for example, how mixed up we became in assuming average arrival and service rates) are so complicated that simulation, with the help of a computer, is almost an essential.

A Simulation Solution to a Waiting-Line Problem

The basic facts are these:

    1. A manufacturing plant has 50 machines.

    2. Machine stoppages occur every 5 to 20 minutes. (All 50 machines are running nicely to start, but every 5 to 20 minutes one machine or another breaks down and needs service).

    3. The plant has fixed production requirements based on the assumption that all machines operate 40 hours per week. Any machine downtime must be made up by working it overtime, which costs $8 per hour.

    4. A repairman costs $5 per hour.

These facts may seem inadequate, but this is the basic type of information a foreman may have on which to base his recommendation as to how many repairmen he should have on his payroll.

The thoughtful foreman will study the problem in detail and find that historically the time interval between stoppages has varied as shown in Table 16–3.

He will also have ascertained that, on the average, repair times vary as shown in Table 16–4.

TABLE 16–3

Time Interval Between Stoppages	Frequency
5 minutes	20%
10 minutes	50%
15 minutes	20%
20 minutes	10%

TABLE 16–4

Service Time	Frequency
10 minutes	20%
15 minutes	50%
20 minutes	20%
25 minutes	10%

It seems pretty clear to him that time to service has no relation to the intervals between stoppages (once again, his managerial judgment). Relying on history, he also sees no reason to believe that future machine operations will result in more or fewer stoppages at very different intervals.

At the same time, he recognizes that, on any given day, he can never predict how frequently stoppages will occur and how long each breakdown will take to service. Some days he wishes he had three times as many repairmen as he has; on other days he burns at the fact he is paying $5 an hour for repairmen sitting idle.

Enter the Operations Research man. After studying all available facts and discussing the problem with the foreman, he suggests the use of Monte Carlo Sampling, a particular kind of simulation. Although this technique is not used in waiting problems alone, its use illustrates how closely interrelated OR techniques are.

Basically, the Monte Carlo Sampling technique suggests that if we have a range of possibilities that occur by chance, we can best predict what will happen by simulating how these chance variations occur. To apply this sampling technique, basing our information on the foreman's study of stoppages, we can take 10 pieces of paper and write

5 on 2 pieces
10 on 5 pieces
15 on 2 pieces
20 on 1 piece

Then if we mix all 10 pieces of paper in a hat and choose 1 blindfolded, we have a fair chance of coming up with what might represent the time interval for the first stoppage. Returning this piece of paper to the hat, we repeat the process. Of course, there are less clumsy ways to do this, but the procedure described demonstrates a method of choosing a possibility in such a way that the probability of choosing it is the same as we would attach to the event actually occurring.

In our particular case, we have used the same technique to determine the frequency of machine stoppages and the time it takes to service each stoppage. Using the Monte Carlo Sampling technique, we come up with the figures shown in Table 16–5.

TABLE 16–5

MONTE CARLO SAMPLING RESULTS

Breakdown	Time Since Last Stoppage	Time to Service Stoppage
1	20	30
2	10	15
3	10	15
4	20	30
5	15	30
6	20	25
7	20	30
8	5	25
9	10	15
10	10	25
11	10	25

The above model, which was chosen to demonstrate a particular technique, covers only 150 minutes of a working day. Actually, this simulation should cover a number of days before much validity could be obtained from our results. As a matter of fact, we might use sampling to determine how many days we should include to get confidence in our results.

Given Table 16–5, it is relatively simple to simulate what would happen if we had one serviceman versus two (see Table 16–6). Even with this minimum of 150 minutes of simulation time, it is evident that the foreman will want more than one serviceman in the plant. With just one repairman, the first 11 machines to break down suffer 565 minutes of waiting time. With 2 repairmen, there is only

TABLE 16–6

COMPARATIVE SIMULATION OF MACHINE BREAKDOWNS AND REPAIRS, ASSUMING ONE REPAIRMAN AVAILABLE AND TWO REPAIRMEN AVAILABLE

Breakdown	Time of Breakdown	Time Repair Begins	Waiting Time	Time Repair Ends	Repairman on Job 1	2	Idle Time of Repairman 1	2	No. Machines in Waiting Line
One repairman									
1	20	20	0	50	x		20		0
2	30	50	20	65	x		0		1
3	40	65	25	80	x		0		2
4	60	80	20	110	x		0		2
5	75	110	35	140	x		0		2
6	95	140	45	165	x		0		2
7	115	165	50	195	x		0		2
8	120	195	75	220	x		0		3
9	130	220	90	235	x		0		4
10	140	235	95	260	x		0		4
11	150	260	110	285	x		0		5
Two repairmen									
1	20	20	0	50	x		20	20	
2	30	30	0	45		x	0	0	
3	40	45	5	60		x	0	0	1
4	60	60	0	90		x	0	0	
5	75	75	0	105	x		25	0	
6	95	95	0	120		x	0	5	
7	115	115	0	145	x		10	0	
8	120	120	0	145		x	0	0	
9	130	145	15	170	x		0	0	1
10	140	145	5	170		x	0	0	2
11	150	170	20	195	x		0	0	1

45 minutes of waiting time, a net improvement of some 520 minutes. To figure out what this means in dollars we find that for 2½ hours of serviceman's time, the plant saves more than 8 hours of overtime machine time. Using the cost data presented earlier, this represents a saving of more than $50 in a mere 2½ hour period.

This conclusion is by no means final. We do not know that 2 men are the optimum, and we need more time for further simulation studies. On the other hand, if a computer is available, we are talking about only a very few minutes of additional time to arrive at the best possible solution.

Further, assuming we do this, we have solved only the very obvious part of the problem. Some other questions might well be asked and the answers might shed considerable light on alternative solutions: Can we buy machines that do not break down as often? Can the Queue Discipline (that is, choice of machines to be repaired based on some factor other than which breaks down first) be changed? Should machine operators be trained to keep their own machines in order?

In this problem, idle time was the main consideration. In other problems involving queuing, the main question may be that of customer service. In these cases the willingness of the customer to wait must be balanced against the cost of additional service facilities and the probability question is: What is the maximum time any given customer might be asked to wait?

Summary

Queuing problems exist in almost any kind of business, and such problems will vary from hour to hour and from day to day. The use of some fairly complicated mathematics involved in Queuing Theory, tied in with both probabilities and simulation of actual situations, can be most helpful in gearing up the service facility to the proper economic level.

17 Statistical Inference

The use of statistical inference in solving business problems involves, among other techniques, both sampling and regression. Before the reader lets these terms throw him, let us recognize that we have already discussed sampling in Chapters 14 and 16, and that regression means simply the statistical association between or among variables. Statistical inference is the process of drawing logical conclusions from statistics on what has happened in the past and what is likely to happen in the future.

To begin with, let us review what we know about sampling.

Sampling

Most businessmen are familiar to some degree with statistical sampling. They have used or observed market research tests. They know of quality control tests. They may also have been exposed to work measurement techniques by means of which "a good day's pay for a good day's work" has been established by sampling job content and worker capacity.

Many, if not most, businessmen are still quite skeptical, however, when it comes to using information based on sampling. To put it bluntly, if sampling techniques produce results contrary to the businessman's preconception, he is likely to question the validity of the sample. If his preconception is based on business judgment reflecting his years of experience as to what works and what does not work, his skepticism may be quite valid; perhaps there was indeed some weakness in the selection of the sample. On the other hand, if, as frequently happens, his preconception is not solidly based, a statistical sample can and should open his eyes and his mind.

True, a statistical sample should be viewed critically (or skeptically, if you like) but it should also be viewed open-mindedly because of the potentially valuable information it can yield.

We use statistical sampling for three reasons: cost, quality, and necessity.

COST. It is patently cheaper to take a sample than to observe a whole population. And under cost, we include time as well as money.

QUALITY. Less understood, but very valid, is the fact that a good sampling technique can produce more accurate results than a biased study of a whole population. A house-to-house survey on any given question using hundreds of unskilled interviewers typically will produce less valid results than a well-constructed sample survey conducted by trained, unbiased interviewers.

NECESSITY. In many cases it is obviously impossible even to contemplate a universal sample. Consider, for example, the quality control problem in which the only workable test involves total destruction of the product. Here sampling is the only practicable answer.

Sampling and Probability

The theory of sampling is based upon the concepts of probability dealt with earlier. If the reader concedes that probability can be helpful in the decision-making process, he should be receptive to the use of sampling. Sampling represents the application of the principles of probability to the problems of accumulating and analyzing information.

Let us assume you have two pails, each holding 100 balls. In pail A you have 80 red balls and 20 blue balls. In pail B you have 20 red balls and 80 blue balls.

Let us further assume that someone (friend or enemy, it does not matter) blindfolds you and puts one of the pails in front of you and suggests that, after thoroughly shaking the pail, you select a ball by chance. The ball you happen to choose turns up red, and you replace it in the pail. After thoroughly shaking the pail again, you choose another ball; it turns out to be red also.

Can you now determine whether you have been selecting from pail A or pail B? The answer is no, but you can be pretty sure that it is pail A. If you went through one more selection and came out with a red ball, you would be even surer.

The odds work out as follows: If you are drawing from pail A, your chance of getting a red ball is .8. Your chance of drawing 2 red balls in a row is .8 × .8, or .64. If you had been drawing from pail B, your initial chance of getting a red ball would have been .2; and of getting two red balls in a row, .2 × .2, or .04—4 chances in 100 as opposed to 64 chances in 100. In other words, you are 16 times more likely to be drawing from pail A than pail B if you draw 2 red balls in a row. These are pretty good odds on which to base a judgment.

Let us continue the experiment. Following the preceding conditions, let us draw 2 more balls from the pail. For purposes of our discussion, let us assume that both these balls are red. Going back to the mathematics expressed above, the chances of this happening if the balls are drawn from pail A are .8 × .8 × .8 × .8, or .4196. In brief, if you are drawing from pail A this should happen over 40 per cent of the time. If you were drawing from pail B, however, the mathematics are .2 × .2 × .2 × .2, or .0016, or less than 2 chances in a thousand.

At this point, unless you are a confirmed long-shot man, you would have to conclude that you have been withdrawing balls from pail A. You could not be certain, but there is a statistical technique which indicates that you would be right 97 per cent of the time if you said you had been drawing from pail A, versus a 3 per cent chance that you were drawing from pail B.

There is no point in going into the equations used in arriving at the 97 to 3 ratio stated above. What is important is to understand sampling. We are saying, first, that from different populations (pail A and pail B) we expect to find the probabilities of drawing a certain sample (4 reds) to differ (.4196 to .0016). Turning this around, we can say that, if we have a sample, we can calculate the probability of that sample coming from different populations (97 per cent from pail A, 3 per cent from pail B). What we are trying to establish is that, by observing our sample we can calculate the true population ratio in terms of probability.

While this example is adequate to make a point, it is rather unreal in that we have only two alternatives, and the answer had to be one or the other. In most business situations, we have no idea what the ratio might be and the choices that face us might range from a very small percentage ratio of red balls to 100 per cent. This fact does not hinder the statistician, because his approach is to assume that there is a broad range of possibilities and his chore is to calculate the probability of each being the true one.

To take another possibly more realistic situation, let us assume we have just one pail of balls, both red and white, and no knowledge of how many balls or how many of which color are in the pail. Let us assume that we follow our previous procedure (blindfold . . . pick . . . replace . . . shake . . . pick again) and come up with 15 red balls and 10 white ones. We have no prior knowledge of the true proportion of reds to whites, but we can say, based upon the mathematics of probability, that there is a 70 per cent probability that the number of red balls is between 50 and 70 per cent of the total population and a 95 per cent probability that the number of red balls lies between 40 and 80 per cent of the population.

Increasing the amount of the sample proportionate to the total will of course lead to increasingly reliable and sharper conclusions.

Assuming that the reader has followed to this point, he may well ask how all this discussion of sampling and probabilities is pertinent to the businessman. In answer, it is undeniable that businesses rise or fall based upon managerial judgments. Whether managers realize it or not, many decisions are based upon the probabilities of future happenings; and techniques which enable the business manager to eliminate personal bias in arriving at judgments can therefore be very helpful.

A word of caution: Sampling yields probabilistic, not absolute, results.

Regression and Correlation

The mathematical definition of regression as "the amount by which the conditional expectation of one of two correlated variables is closer to the mean of its set than are given values of the second to the mean of its set" is of relatively little help to most businessmen. Nevertheless, the use of regression analysis can be most helpful in the use of statistical inference to solve business problems.

To get away from the gobbledygook of the preceding paragraph, let us simply say that the use of regression analysis is one of observing past data, equating varying conditions in effect at the times these data were produced, and groping for some correlation which may be helpful in projecting future results.

Most typically we are looking for cause-and-effect relationships. Does an increase in earnings cause an increase in the price of a stock, and, if so, when and by how much? Does an increase in numbers of marriages presage greater demand for housing, and, if so, what time lag is involved? It can readily be seen that where specific cause-and-effect relationships exist, planning for business decisions is much easier.

A Business Example

A sales manager is running into quite a bit of price competition in selling a line of widgets. His product is good, but not demonstrably better than his competitors'. He comes to the production manager and asks how low a price he can set on widgets and still make a reasonable profit for his company. The production manager has kept good cost records, but finds that his direct manufacturing costs for widgets have varied fairly substantially in recent months. For example, while labor, material, and overhead costs have been stable, the last 10 batches of widgets showed the unit costs given in Table 17-1.

TABLE 17-1

Batch No.	Direct Cost per Unit
1	$5.00
2	4.70
3	4.60
4	4.90
5	4.10
6	4.40
7	4.30
8	4.80
9	4.50
10	4.20

Hence, he says his average unit cost, based on total production for the 10 batches, is $4.55, but he recognizes that giving the cost figure to the sales manager might well be misleading because of the variations in costs involved in comparing one batch to another. Assuming these last 10 batches are representative, costs will vary up to 10 per cent more or less. In the low-margin widget business, he recognizes that he should be more accurate both in prediction and in cost performance.

After considerable thought, he suddenly realizes that the major variable influencing unit costs might well be the size of batch manufactured at any given time. So he decides to test this theory. Batch sizes of these 10 batches were as shown in Table 17–2.

TABLE 17–2

Batch No.	Number of Units
1	200
2	500
3	600
4	300
5	1,100
6	800
7	900
8	400
9	700
10	1,000

He then draws a graph comparing cost per batch (on the vertical scale) with batch size (on the horizontal scale). See Figure 17–1.

At this juncture, he is jubilant. A straight line can be drawn through all the points. He can tell the sales manager that, if he is told how many widgets to make, he can predict direct cost right

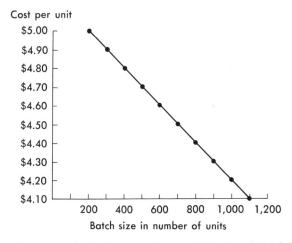

Figure 17–1. Correlation Between Cost per Widget and Batch Size

on the head. All uncertainty in working with averages has disappeared. Based upon this graph, he can be completely accurate in cost predictions if he knows how many widgets to make.

Uses of Regression Analysis and Correlation

Of course, our reader knows that things never work out this smoothly in real life, but this simple example does give a good example of the use of regression analysis and correlation.

The "best fit" curve drawn on this graph is a regression line. In this case the curve was a straight line. In most cases it is very unlikely that the "best fit" will go through all the points, primarily because other variables creep in. Suppose Old Ben, who operates the drill press on a major widget-producing operation, comes to work with a hangover. Or suppose there were flaws in the metal used in the raw material for widgets. It is easy to identify many other factors which can influence production and costs and prevent such a lovely, simple solution.

Moreover, with the introduction of more variables (fixed costs as well as direct costs, for example) the best fit will become a curve rather than a straight line. And as we increase the numbers of variables, we reach the point where the answers cannot be reflected on a graph and the analyst must state and solve his problem through increasingly complicated mathematical formulas. Despite all these added complexities, however, the idea of the regression function is as demonstrated above; it establishes a relationship among variables, and depending upon how good a fit this "best fit" function is, it improves our guessing power in assessing future situations. The "best fit" line is determined by how well it will accurately describe and possibly predict what has happened and is likely to happen in the future.

The question of how good a fit the regression function is depends upon how much uncertainty it eliminates. In our simple example, knowledge of batch size eliminates all uncertainty as to cost per unit. Without knowledge of batch size, the best we could say is that cost per unit averages $4.55 and that it will vary around this amount by as much as plus or minus 10 per cent but with uncertainty. Knowing batch size explains all variations, so that we can say that the regression function which relates batch size to cost per unit is a very good fit.

The mathematical criterion that tells how good a fit the regression function is is called the coefficient of determination. It tells us how much of the variation in one variable can be explained by knowledge of another variable. In this case, the coefficient of determination is 100 per cent because 10 per cent of the variation in cost per unit is explained by knowledge of batch size. (In the event you run into the term "coefficient of correlation," do not be disturbed. It is merely the square root of the coefficient of determination, and basically tells you the same thing in more sophisticated problems).

A More Practical Situation

We have already indicated that you rarely find a coefficient of determination of 100 per cent because other variables occur, sometimes on a chance basis. It is helpful, however, to isolate a principal variable, if only to see what other variables cause different results.

Just to lend some reality to prove our point, let us assume that a restaurateur undertakes a study of the raw-food cost of French fried potatoes served to his customers. We also assume that he serves these potatoes, family style, with a bowl placed in the center of the table to serve an entire party. Through his own devious

TABLE 17–3

Number in Party	Raw Cost of Potatoes Served
2	$.02
3	.04
4	.03
5	.04
5	.06
6	.06
7	.07
7	.08
9	.08

means, he calculates the raw cost of potatoes served to nine different parties of people over a period of time with the results shown in Table 17–3.

Graphing the above figures, we obtain Figure 17–2:

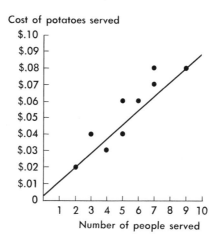

Figure 17–2. Correlation Between Cost of Potatoes and Number of People Served

Here, when the best-fit regression line is drawn, we see the more typical result: most of the situations tend to cluster in the neighborhood of this line, but are not exactly on it. In this example we know that the major variable affecting the cost of potatoes served must be the number of people served, and we can establish mathematically that the coefficient of determination here is 84.5 per cent. What this means is that 84.5 per cent of the variation in cost is explained by the number of people being served.

Knowledge of this fact can be extremely helpful to us in that we can now concentrate our management efforts on variations from this norm; in effect, we isolate the major variable (number of people being served) and worry about other variables (kitchen spoilage, serving too large portions, staff eating habits, etc.)

Summary

When the coefficient of determination is 100 per cent, we can say that the dependent variable is the only cause of variation in the independent variable. As the coefficient of determination declines, however, we are forced to realize that there are other variables at work, and we must isolate them to determine their effects. Lower values of the coefficient of determination may mean either of the following:

1. There are other significant variables which should be isolated and measured.

2. There are many small factors, none of which is significant in itself, which are not susceptible to isolation and measurement from a practical viewpoint.

Great care is necessary at this point. All we are measuring is association in an attempt to establish cause-and-effect relationships. Even when the coefficient of determination is very high, it could be that what we are seeing is not a cause-and-effect relationship but rather two variables that are associated by some common cause or causes which we have not considered. For example, the medical profession has established a strong relationship between cigarette smoking and heart disease, but who knows whether cigarette smoking causes heart disease or whether a person prone to heart disease is also likely to be a heavy smoker, with both of these tendencies due to some third factor? Also, it is possible to find nonsense correlations which can occur by chance. Unless a manager can see or find valid reasons for a correlation to exist, esoteric correlations should be discarded.

This chapter has merely skimmed the surface of the use of statistical inference. Regression analyses, in particular, can deal with nonlinear relationships, relating many variables. Computer facilities now offer "canned" programs for regression analysis; in mere seconds managers can test relationships among variables which they think might be meaningful.

18 Mathematical Programming

Of all the Operations Research tools, the best known to most businessmen is probably mathematical programming, or at any rate the branch called linear programming.

There are a number of types of mathematical programming, including integer programming, quadratic programming, stochastic programming, dynamic programming, and others.

Based upon proven useful business applications, linear programming is certainly the most important of the group. Actually, the other forms of mathematical programming have developed to overcome some of its limitations, and to a considerable extent are unproven from a practical standpoint.

In mentioning limitations, we certainly do not want to underrate linear programming, which has proved an extremely useful analytical tool in many business situations. Some ten years ago a list of 257 different business applications was published; today such a list would be at least twice as long.

To take a good look at what linear programming is and how it works, it is useful to review the basic idea behind the use of mathematical models as an aid to business decision making. Throughout our discussion of Operations Research, we have tried to establish that the use of mathematical models makes possible a level of complex analysis which could not otherwise be achieved. The retentive, objective, consistent, logical capacities of mathematical models permit analyses of situations which are too complex (that is, have too many interacting variables) for the mind to comprehend unassisted. Mathematical techniques do not provide additional raw data. They do provide a means of treating data to furnish valuable suggestions and conclusions.

In order to perform a valuable mathematical analysis, a real situation must be carefully defined, abstracted, quantified, and restricted as to the number of important variables. Thus, the mathematical analysis almost never analyzes a real problem, but rather a simplified, somewhat unrealistic version of it. This does not negate the value of the information the analysis develops, but it does mean that the manager must be able to put the information into perspective. He must also be alert for other variables which may have been overlooked when quantifying the problem. The information obtained through mathematical programming can be extremely useful in the hands of skilled management.

In mathematical analysis, as in accounting in general, the value of available information depends upon the user's recognition of its limitations. Without accounting information, any manager is lost when it comes to arriving at major planning and control decisions. With it he can gain valuable insight into cause-and-effect relationships and how they affect the efficiency of the company's operations. But he can do this only if he can recognize the limitations of the information available to him.

We reiterate that the position of the intelligent manager is not threatened by increasing use of higher mathematics and the computer. Mathematical formulas often oversimplify, as they must to be effective. They exchange complete realism for simplicity, and are expressed only in quantitative terms, whereas some aspects of problems will always be qualitative and withstand quantitative judgments.

Having said all this, it is still true that mathematical programming can make possible a form of analysis which, because of sheer volume of information to be processed, would otherwise be impossible of comprehension without mathematical tools.

What Is Mathematical Programming?

Typically, mathematical programming deals with finding an optimal (best) allocation of scarce resources. And this is a big part of what business is all about. Most businesses have insufficient capital, for example, to do everything they would like to do; and they must, accordingly, pick and choose the manner in which available funds can best be used. Plant capacity also can be devoted to production of a variety of products. How can it be set up to produce maximum effectiveness? In most situations, management faces a fairly wide choice of alternatives in determining the best way to operate the business.

This kind of problem permeates the structure of many business organizations, from the very top level (deciding where to concentrate capital) to the foreman (deciding how to get maximum productivity out of the line workers).

Mathematical programming is a useful technique for analyzing which of many courses might best maximize the use of scarce resources. Although one example of linear programming has been given in Chapter 12, it may be helpful to run through another case in somewhat more detail.

A Common Shipping Problem

In this case we assume that the Huber Electric Company stocks hundreds of items in 5 warehouses, strategically located in various parts of the United States. Orders are received in one central dispatching office, and requests for shipment are teletyped to the respective warehouses each day by clerks, each of whom handle a sizable number of items. Each clerk has a perpetual inventory record of the number of pieces of each item for which he is responsible, which he keeps up to date. It is each clerk's responsibility to receive orders for the items under his control and to determine which warehouse should ship each item. His judgment is based upon the stocks available at each warehouse, but he must also attempt to minimize shipping costs and achieve fastest delivery.

On a given day, Rita receives 7 orders for a total of 26 of fixture 301, one of the items under her control. These orders break down as shown in Table 18–1.

TABLE 18–1

Customer	No. of Fixture 301 Ordered
A	3
B	1
C	5
D	2
E	4
F	8
G	3
Total	26

She checks her perpetual inventory and finds that (to make the problem simpler, and among other things, avoid the complication of back orders) there are exactly 26 of Fixture 301 in stock in the five warehouses, as shown in Table 18–2.

Since her standing instructions are to ship from the warehouse to the customer as cheaply as possible, she checks her rate schedule and finds that the dollar per unit cost of shipping from each warehouse to each customer is as shown in Table 18–3.

TABLE 18–2

Warehouse No.	No. of Fixture 301 on Hand
1	4
2	6
3	8
4	3
5	5
Total	26

TABLE 18-3

From Warehouse	To Customer						
	A	B	C	D	E	F	G
1	$10	$ 8	$ 5	$ 7	$16	$17	$13
2	17	15	7	4	11	11	8
3	21	19	10	5	5	6	8
4	20	17	8	6	7	10	15
5	14	11	9	11	16	20	22

It should be pretty clear that, given these facts, we have a problem which can be solved mathematically. To use OR jargon, we can reach an optimal solution, one which will minimize our shipping costs of scarce resources. The reader may wonder why we say "scarce resources" when, by the very terms of our problem, we have enough No. 301 fixtures to fill all customer orders. The answer is that, economically, there is a scarcity in that there are not enough No. 301 fixtures in the right places to ship each order from the closest warehouse.

If we had unlimited inventories at each warehouse, our shipping problem would be very simple and the orders might be filled in the fashion shown in Table 18-4.

TABLE 18-4

From Warehouse	To Customer							
	A	B	C	D	E	F	G	Total
1	3	1	5	—	—	—	—	9
2	—	—	—	2	—	—	—	2
3	—	—	—	—	4	8	3	15
4	—	—	—	—	—	—	—	—
5	—	—	—	—	—	—	—	—
Total								26

But, we have earlier pointed out that warehouse 1, for example, has only 4 No. 301 fixtures, while warehouse 3 has 8 fixtures on hand. In short, there are insufficient inventories at the warehouses closest to the customers to provide the cheapest shipping costs. It should now be clear that scarcity does enter into our problem.

Let us take a look at various ways Rita might attempt to solve this problem.

1. Assuming she is responsible for 150 different items in the product line, of which No. 301 is just one, the mail is heavy, and she has an equally heavy date that night, she might figure that the quickest way to get her job done and still satisfy all customer demands would be to fill all orders from available inventories by exhausting warehouse supplies through giving Customer A all he needs from Warehouse 1, satisfying Customer B from Warehouse 1, Customer C from Warehouse 2, and so forth. On this basis the distribution would break down as shown in Table 18–5.

TABLE 18–5

From Warehouse	To Customer							
	A	B	C	D	E	F	G	Total
1	3	1	—	—	—	—	—	4
2	—	—	5	1	—	—	—	6
3	—	—	—	1	4	3	—	8
4	—	—	—	—	—	3	—	3
5	—	—	—	—	—	2	3	5
Total demand	3	1	5	2	4	8	3	26

By referring to Table 18–3, we can calculate that the cost of this solution to our problem is $266. This is a solution, but very unlikely to be the cheapest solution.

2. If Rita had a little more time, she might look at a map and try to figure a better way to solve the problem. Based on her best guess as to how to match up shipping points with customer locations, she might come up with a pattern like that in Table 18–6.

Applying the rates shown in Table 18–3, it is clear that this is a much better answer in that total shipping costs are $220, a saving of $46 over her first try.

By further use of trial-and-error judgment, and considerable expenditure of time, Rita might work down to an even better solution. But by use of a relatively simple mathematical formula, she can calculate by hand in about 5 minutes (mere seconds on a

TABLE 18-6

From Warehouse	To Customer							
	A	B	C	D	E	F	G	Total Supply
1	—	—	4	—	—	—	—	4
2	—	—	1	2	—	—	3	6
3	—	—	—	—	4	4	—	8
4	—	—	—	—	—	3	—	3
5	3	1	—	—	—	1	—	5
Total demand	3	1	5	2	4	8	3	26

computer) what the very best solution is. In this case the optimum solution is as shown in Table 18–7.

The total cost of our optimum solution is $193. Certainly this saving over the previous solutions is worth 5 minutes of Rita's time. Also, by applying the mathematical formula to this problem, you *know* that you are shipping the very cheapest way possible.

TABLE 18-7

From Warehouse	To Customer							
	A	B	C	D	E	F	G	Total Supply
1	3	—	1	—	—	—	—	4
2	—	—	—	2	—	1	3	6
3	—	—	—	—	1	7	—	8
4	—	—	—	—	3	—	—	3
5	—	1	4	—	—	—	—	5
Total demand	3	1	5	2	4	8	3	26

Throughout this book, we have made our examples fairly simple to establish each point as we go along. Obviously, supply and demand are rarely in exact balance; there may be ten times as many warehouses and customers; timing may be so important that it is desirable to ship by air from a more distant point to get faster delivery; and there may be many other variables to consider. All we are trying to stress here is that it is valuable to have a mathematical technique which produces an optimal allocation which you know to be the best possible solution. And such techniques have been developed to handle many more variables than appear in our sample problem, and are in use today.

The Logic of Mathematical Programming

The very purpose of this book would be destroyed if we went deeply into the formulas used in mathematical programming, but it might be useful to understand the logic behind the mathematics employed.

In Rita's second solution (Table 18–6), let us pay particular attention to the shipments from Warehouses 3 and 4 to Customers E and F, as shown in Table 18–8.

TABLE 18–8

From	To Customer		
Warehouse	E	F	Total
3	4	4	8
4	—	3	3
Total	4	7	11

Using the rate schedule in Table 18–3, we see that the per unit shipping rates are as follows:

From Warehouse 3 to Customer E, $5
From Warehouse 3 to Customer F, $6
From Warehouse 4 to Customer E, $7
From Warehouse 4 to Customer F, $10

It is apparent that every unit now being shipped to Customer E from Warehouse 3 which is transferred to Customer F costs the Huber Company an additional dollar. At the same time, every unit being shipped from Warehouse 4 which is moved to Customer E, rather than Customer F, saves the company $3. If an arrangement can be worked out so that more items are shipped from Warehouse 4 to Customer E, even at the increased expense of shipping from Warehouse 3 to Customer F, each pair of items interchanged in this manner saves the company $2. You will note that in the optimal solution (Table 18–7) this switch has been made.

As this example indicates, mathematical programming is a

technique that searches for this type of profitable substitution, and the solution reached by a well-programmed model is one in which all profitable substitutions have been made. That is, the optimal solution has been reached.

Mathematical programming, although it may involve higher mathematics, is simply a routine, though sometimes a complicated one. When we realize this, it becomes clear that the most important part of the operation is in the statement of the problem so that the equations can be properly structured. In the problem outlined above, for example, if the real question were the problem of fastest, rather than cheapest, delivery, the answer might be totally different. Further, perhaps the bigger problem is, "How many warehouses should Huber have?" Mathematical programming can help the able manager improve his performance, but it is not about to replace him.

Basic Features of Mathematical Programming

Every mathematical program consists of three factors: (1) the decision variables, (2) the objective function, and (3) the constraints. Lest all this sound like gobbledygook, let's relate these criteria to our shipping problem.

1. *The decision variables* are the actual allocations, in this case the number of items to be shipped from each warehouse to each customer. In the statement of the problem, they are the unknowns whose optimal values we are trying to determine.

2. *The objective function* is the criterion by which we define optimum. In our example, we have stated our objective function as minimizing the cost of shipping. As pointed out earlier, it might well be that the wrong question is being asked, and delivery time may be more important than cost, but in our case we have said that shipping cost is to be minimized and, accordingly, this is the objective function.

3. *The constraints* are the scarce resources, in this case the inventories at each of the warehouses.

To put all these together, every mathematical programming problem can be described as one in which the goal is to define the decision variables so as to minimize (or maximize, as the case may be) the objective function, given the constraints of the situation.

Applications of Mathematical Programming

Every reader can think of some practical application of mathematical programming to his own business. The following examples should accustom the reader to the terms used so that he can define his own problems.

1. THE PRODUCT-MIX PROBLEM. The manager must decide how much of each of a number of products to produce when productive capacity must be allocated. Typically, various raw materials may be used, and various finished products turned out. Examples range from oil refineries to machine shops.

The decision variables are the materials to be used (in the case of oil refineries, varieties of crude oil; in the case of machine shops, varieties of fabricated metals). The objective function is the maximization of profit by producing the most profitable product lines. The constraints are which materials (crude oil, types of fabricated metals) are available.

2. THE ASSIGNMENT-OF-ORDERS PROBLEM. A company has a number of factories, each of which could produce the product for a given order. To which plant or plants should the order be assigned?

The decision variables are the orders received. The objective function is the maximization of profit from all plants. The constraints are availability of raw materials, shipping costs in and out, and factory capacity and unit cost.

3. THE "TRIM WASTE"-IN-A-PAPER-MILL PROBLEM. While seemingly a rather parochial situation, this one is cited because it has facets similar to many other businesses in that best use of available facilities is involved. Here the problem is to make best use, with minimum waste, of giant paper machines in filling customers' orders.

The decision variables, once again, are the orders received (or the desirability of producing stock for future sales from inventory). The objective function (this is becoming increasingly clearer) is the maximization of profit from operations by minimizing costs. The constraints are the capacity of the paper-making machine or machines and the widths of paper stock available. In this case the basic problem is determining how the otherwise wasted width and length of a continuous roll of paper can be reduced by rescheduling runs so that the maximum use can be made of each run. One major paper company has reported an increase in trim efficiency of 1.5 per cent through use of linear programming, or the equivalent of 15 more tons of usable production per day.

Limitations and Complications

Mathematical programming can indeed be most useful to the business manager, but now let us wave some danger flags concerning its limitations and complications. We have defined this technique as one for determining optimal allocation of scarce resources. From this it might appear that most business decisions are amenable to mathematical programming analysis, since so many of these decisions are attempts to solve problems involving optimizing profits under conditions of scarcity of one kind or another. The practical stumbling block is in the limitations of the technique.

As mentioned before, most practical mathematical programming to date has been in linear programming. By definition, linear programming requires that all relationships be linear. This means that for every unit change in the decision variable, the objective function must change by the same amount. For example, if we say that costs increase $1 for every extra part No. 301 produced, this must hold true whether we are talking about the first extra part or the one hundred and first. If this is not true, either because of economies of scale or diminishing returns, or for some other reason, the relationship is no longer lineal, and the linear programming analysis means less. In business most relationships are nonlinear. Although there are techniques already developed and being developed to overcome this limitation, the state of the art in dealing with non-linear problems is less than commercially successful.

Moreover, mathematical programming models are basically deterministic, in that they do not take into account uncertainty. A technique called stochastic programming has been developed to deal with uncertainty, but most sophisticated businessmen still prefer to take the deterministic results generated by linear programming, using their judgment to qualify them and to reshape their actions after taking uncertainties into account.

Also, most mathematical models are static, in that they do not incorporate dynamic (changing) features that characterize most business problems. By this we mean that most programming is designed to determine what the optimum was yesterday, might be today, but may not be tomorrow. The alert manager is interested not only in today's optimum, but that which will optimize over the long pull. Unfortunately, however, managers are often judged, and recognize they are being judged, on current results rather than on development for the future.

In short, current business emphasis on immediate results has militated heavily against production of long-range planning techniques which produce suboptimal results currently. Attempts have been made to program for the future by dealing with nonlinear relationships, but this so-called dynamic programming has produced little of a proven, practical nature.

The most difficult part of the use of mathematical programming is the setting up of a workable mathematical model. This requires bringing into the picture a man with training in mathematics. But the mathematician often does not understand business, and the businessman does not understand mathematics; so they do not understand each other and any potential project fails. In other cases, the mathematician is charmed with formulas and "plowing new fields" which are incomprehensible to the layman. The "feeling out" process between the businessman and the mathematician may well take a long time and be quite costly from the standpoint of computer usage.

In those cases where the businessman knows what is important and can get this across to the mathematician, the mathematician is willing to accept value judgments on items that are not quantifiable, and the businessman and the mathematician can work as an effective team, major steps forward can be taken through mathematical programming. When results are obtained, there is still a considerable business judgment to be applied in being sure that all major factors have been considered and any limitations on the scope of the activity have been recognized.

Summary

Mathematical programming has proved to be the most useful Operations Research technique for getting better answers to business problems. It has been applied to a wide assortment of different situations, but most typically it is used to determine the best allocation of resources.

No company has infinite resources. The use of mathematical programming can be very helpful in examining alternative uses of resources to establish how to get the most out of what a company has.

19 Critical Path Scheduling

Complicated scheduling problems have been the source of many headaches to Operations Research practitioners. The constantly changing problems involved in sequencing a number of activities over varying amounts of manpower, machine and time capacities have to date proved too difficult for the mathematics of optimization. Except for fairly simple scheduling situations, OR men have had to rely on simulation techniques to deal with sequencing problems. Under this condition, successful results are occasionally achieved, but not so frequently that businessmen readily turn to Operations Research to handle their scheduling problems.

As a result, most businessmen handle complicated scheduling problems by a combination of trial and error and the educated guess. Production-control visual aids such as Gantt Charts (see Figure 19-1) have been in use for some time. Although helpful, they can hardly be considered any breakthrough.

There are certain specific types of scheduling problems, however, which are solvable by the use of mathematical techniques. In a number of one-of-a-kind scheduling projects, the solutions can be quite dramatic and useful. As usual, these techniques have acquired an aura of complexity and mystery.

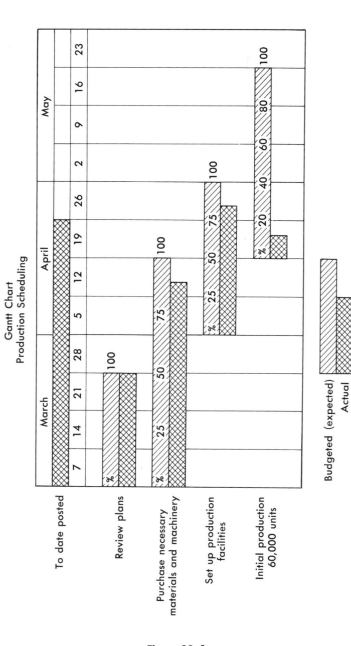

Figure 19–1

These techniques, the best known being PERT and CPM, can be complex, but the ideas behind them are relatively simple.

PERT and CPM

PERT (Project Evaluation and Review Technique) and CPM (Critical Path Measurement) are similar techniques used in the planning and control of one-of-a-kind operations, such as the development and production of a new project. Both techniques came into prominence in the late 1950s in connection with work being done for the Defense Department and have proved to be efficient aids to management in both government contracts and industry problems.

Although PERT and CPM are basically the same technique, and we shall refer to them as PERT-CPM, they differ in approach. In essence, PERT takes into account uncertainty in estimating completion of activity while CPM uses the single "most likely" time as the best estimate. Thus, typically the application of CPM is somewhat less complicated than that of PERT but may or may not bring about as happy a result.

One-of-a-Kind Projects

The phrase "one of a kind" means nonrepetitive projects, problems which have not been solved before. It appears that with increasing technological breakthroughs our economy faces an increasing number of such problems. A few areas where these techniques can be helpful are: missile-development projects (PERT came to prominence in connection with the Polaris missile); programs to bring a commercial product from research to mass distribution; training programs including the incorporation of learning curves; major construction projects; development programs for undeveloped countries.

There is a pattern of need—certain common problems to be

208 | Planning and Control for Profit

solved—in connection with areas susceptible to PERT-CPM application. The prime factors are these:

1. There is a time objective, in that it is desirable to reach a specific point by a certain time, and usually there is a penalty for being late.

2. A number of different activities must be completed before the final completion of the project.

3. Typically, some activities in the chain of events cannot be started until others have been completed, and some activities can be worked on simultaneously while others are progressing.

4. The cost of completing each activity is to some extent dependent on how much time can be allowed to complete it. If overtime must be worked, or larger crews of less trained workers must be brought in to meet a deadline, the job must cost more. On the other hand, costs can be cut if the time for each activity is planned so well that it can be pursued in the cheapest way.

The aim in this kind of problem is clear—to finish the project on time at the lowest cost possible. The key decisions the manager faces are to decide at what point in time each activity should be started to ensure smooth coordination of all things to be done, to have advance knowledge of the bottlenecks on which his resources must be concentrated, and to allocate his resources as efficiently as possible.

This kind of problem is almost never a static one. The facts are always changing (for example, a key man who appears irreplaceable has a heart attack; some obscure union goes on strike; faulty components are delivered). But by planning what has to be done, and by when, the manager is in a position to control his final output by shifting his resources to meet new bottlenecks as they arise.

It should be evident that planning and controlling a large project is a major job. Hundreds of things are being worked on at the same time. Finishing one project has to dovetail with many others. One slip can hold up the entire operation. The usefulness of a technique that can compress this job into manageable proportions must be obvious.

Up to this point we have been talking about PERT-CPM in general terms. Let us now apply it to a business situation.

A Practical Problem

The Vincent Toy Company has a well-respected name for imaginative, quality products. Its bread-and-butter line is toys for which there is a continuing demand, year after year, but to keep its position in the field it must not only update and repackage its proven items, but also come up with new products which create new demand each year. Because of the Christmas season, 70 per cent of its sales are made in August and September, and if distributors are not fully stocked by October 1, substantial sales will be lost.

During the latter part of May, one of Vincent's kooky inventors with whom it has been dealing for a number of years comes in with a working model of a walking doll which not only turns away from obstacles in her way but does dance steps in perfect time. The marketing people are enthusiastic; the production men and accountants agree that she can be made at a price which should return an excellent profit. But if the Christmas market this year is lost, some other company may come out with a comparable product and "Dancing Della" would be just another competitive item.

Enter the Operations Research man. After studying the problem, he says that based on normal operating procedures, Vincent can deliver Dancing Della to distributors in quantity by October 15 if it meets the time schedule shown in Table 19–1.

To arrive at the October 15 date, the OR man has prepared a PERT network, a visual representation (a graphic model rather than a mathematical one) of all the activities and events that go into the project, drawn to show the order in which activities would normally progress. His first PERT network is shown in Figure 19–2.

In this figure the activities listed in Table 19–1 are represented by arrows and are numbered to match. The beginning and ending of these activities are represented by boxes identified by letters. The

TABLE 19–1

Activity	Activity Description	Time Expected to Complete	Must be Preceded by Action No.
1	Obtain raw materials	3 weeks	
2	Set up machinery	5 weeks	
3	Design package	4 weeks	
4	Outline campaign to salesmen	5 weeks	
5	Produce body of doll	2 weeks	1, 2
6	Produce machinery for doll	3 weeks	1, 2
7	Assemble complete doll	2 weeks	5, 6
8	Set up packaging machinery	5 weeks	3
9	Obtain packaging materials	3 weeks	3
10	Prepare promotion materials	3 weeks	3
11	Sell distributors	10 weeks	4, 10
12	Package	1 week	7, 8, 9
13	Ship to distributors	1 week	11, 12

so-called dummy activities, represented by broken lines, merely define relationships of precedence and should be considered activities that consume no resources or time.

From Figure 19–2, we can read, for example, that activity 12, packaging, can begin only at K, after activities 7, 8, and 9 have been completed, which is at the end of the tenth week.

Drawing the network is a simple chore once the activities and relationships of precedence have been defined. The real job is getting the facts together and arranging them. This requires knowledge of what makes up the project in great detail and is a real managerial function. This function, examining each piece of the operation as an entity, and fitting it into its place, frequently results in the discovery of new, better, and quicker ways to get the job done.

The Critical Path

Once the network has been set up, the expected completion time can be determined. In our case, the critical path is as follows:

$$A \text{ to } F \text{ to } J \text{ to } M \text{ to } N$$
or
$$4 \text{ weeks} + 3 \text{ weeks} + 10 \text{ weeks} + 1 \text{ week} = 18 \text{ weeks}$$

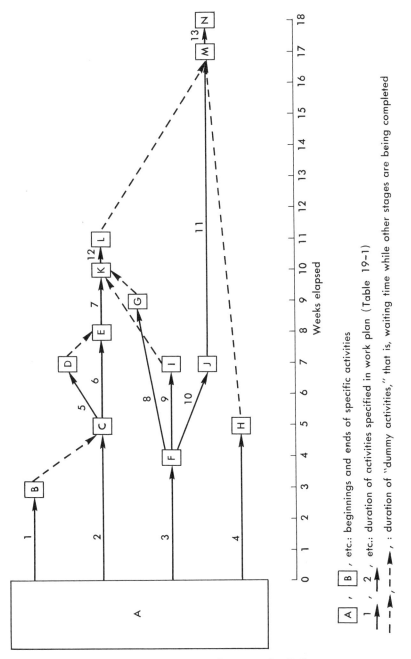

Figure 19–2. PERT Network for Dancing Della

A , B , etc.: beginnings and ends of specific activities

1 , 2 , etc.: duration of activities specified in work plan (Table 19–1)

—▸ ---▸ : duration of "dummy activities," that is, waiting time while other stages are being completed

Dancing Della cannot be in the distributors' hands until activities 3, 10, 11, and 13 (Figure 19–2) have been completed; since each must follow the other, it will take 18 weeks to get the job done.

We call this path the critical path because any delay in activities on this path would cause a delay in the whole project. On the other side of the picture, if we want to speed up the project, it is activities on this path that must be worked on first.

The activities not on this path (for example, activity 8, setting up packaging machinery) are said to have some slack in them, in that they could be stretched out in time without affecting the completion date of the project. If we went through the mathematics involved, we would see that although activity 8 is only supposed to take 5 weeks, it could be stretched to 12 weeks if either necessary or desirable, without affecting the 18-week completion date. This is true in varying degrees of all the activities not on the critical path, and it will not help us to speed up these activities in trying to shorten over-all completion time.

The critical path concept is a simple one: find the areas critical to the timing of the project and speed them up. In practice, however, PERT-CPM problems can be terribly complex when thousands of activities have to be coordinated efficiently. In a large system it is quite easy to mistake slack variables for critical ones and to waste considerable time and money on the wrong problems. Where problems are of substantial size, advanced mathematics and computers can be extremely helpful, but the theory is basically as above described.

Cost and Other Factors

Meanwhile, back at the Vincent Toy Company, we have a problem. Our critical path says it will take 18 weeks to get Dancing Della into the distributors' hands, and we know that we will miss a sizable chunk of the Christmas business unless this time span can be shortened to 16 weeks.

Our critical path shows that the following items should be concentrated on in any attempt to reduce the required time (see Table 19–2):

TABLE 19–2

Activity	Description	Time Expected to Complete
3	Design package	4 weeks
10	Prepare promotion materials	3 weeks
11	Sell distributors	10 weeks
13	Ship to distributors	1 week
Total		18 weeks

In trying to meet a desired timetable, it is often possible to come up with alternative possible actions to save the desired time, each of which is costed out, and the one that costs the least is selected. The manager cannot rely completely on the sharpness of his pencil, however, but must take into consideration qualitative judgments as well as quantitative ones.

In the Vincent case, for example, it is logical to look at the critical path activities and attack first activity 11—the process of selling distributors—because it has the longest time span and, hence, the saving of any given percentage of time would yield the greatest saving in number of days. In this case, however, we find that the promotion of Dancing Della comes at the salesmen's busiest time of the year, when the salesmen are booking their Christmas business for the entire line. There are just 10 Vincent salesmen, each with a geographic territory, and each is known and respected by his distributors. Adding more salesmen would disrupt morale since a sizable portion of each salesman's income depends on the business he brings in. After considerable thought, Vincent's sales manager states that he cannot see any way to cut the 10-week time for selling distributors appreciably, without taking chances of causing irreparable harm to the continuing sales effort of the Vincent Toy Company.

In the meantime, the shipping manager has been working on the problem of trying to reduce the one-week time for shipments. Based upon a combination of split shipments and last-minute shipments by air, he finds that he can save 3 days in the schedule at a cost of about $12,000, based upon expected sales for Dancing Della.

When he was originally approached for his best estimate on time, the chief design engineer estimated 4 weeks for package design, a very major function for Vincent because prominence of display and attractiveness of packaging is so important in the impulse purchase of toys. When the critical path study indicated that he should be approached again to see if the 4-week period could be cut back, he hit the ceiling, pointing out that he and his department were now working excessive overtime, had not had their full vacations and did not expect to get them, and just could not be asked to work any harder. Since the man was greatly respected in the trade as a near genius, Mr. Vincent, the president, calmed him down, told him how much he was appreciated, and gently mentioned, as he was leaving the office, how important it was to the company to save 2 weeks in getting Dancing Della out to the trade. The following morning the chief design engineer was in Mr. Vincent's office to tell him that he had been in touch with the Babcock Package Design Company the preceding evening, spent 4 hours with Bernie Babcock giving him his ideas as to packaging Dancing Della, and been assured that Bernie could come up with a "pretty fair" (a high accolade) design in 2 weeks at a cost of $5,000. He assured Mr. Vincent that he could personally find time to make any minor alterations to Babcock's design which he felt necessary as the project went on.

Mr. Vincent also, as a matter of routine, visited his promotion manager, who had initially estimated 3 weeks' production time for promotion materials. There he found that due to a recently settled printers' strike, his promotion manager was barely holding his own by authorizing overtime at Vincent's expense. His happy news was that he had added another qualified supplier to his list, and that could get the promotion materials out on the 3-week schedule promised by paying $2,500 in overtime, but that he saw no way to speed up production at any cost.

With anticipated gross profits of $100,000 on Dancing Della in her first year, Mr. Vincent's decision was now clear. After examination of the critical path revealed that speeding up the package-design operation had no effect on other critical operations, he authorized a $5,000 contract to the Babcock Package Design activity, thus shortening the total time span for Dancing Della to the desired 16 weeks. Shortly thereafter, he issued "stretch-out" orders on slack activities where money could be saved thereby. He also insisted on weekly progress reports on each activity to be sure that no slippage occurred.

Summary

The advantages of using PERT-CMP in the planning stages are these:

1. A plan is set up that makes it easy to see problems in advance, and to anticipate bottlenecks before they appear on the scene.

2. The user is enabled to choose a project plan that most economically achieves the time objective desired, including both adding cost where necessary, and reducing costs where possible within the framework.

The PERT-CMP framework helps control the program in two ways.

1. It makes possible the establishment of time and cost standards by which performance can be judged.

2. If unanticipated delays develop, it facilitates calculation of the revised critical path and defines what is the most economic reallocation of resources.

20   The Usefulness of Operations Research
in Planning and Control

It is trite to say that we are living in a rapidly changing world, but the businessman had better believe it. In addition to the many new machines, which most businessmen find they can understand, there are also new ways of doing things, many of which are based upon mathematical analysis. How much the businessman or manager must know to take advantage of new tools available to him is the big question. It should be obvious that there is a considerable gap between existing knowledge which could be used and that which is being used, and this gap is widening.

As of now, the businessman-manager has three options in choosing the manner in which he will operate.

1. He may "fly by the seat of the pants," using intuition (which should never be underestimated, in that it is often the result of distilled information and experience—the automatic recognition of circumstances which have occurred before, and a quick reaction as to how to behave). Under this type of management, the bright young subordinate is likely to chafe, and wonder how the "old man" can be so lucky. Nevertheless, many, if not most, large businesses have been built in this manner.

2. He may make use of modern management techniques with-

out having in-depth knowledge of exactly how they work. This is the kind of manager for whom this book is written. Most of us who drive cars have only a vague idea of what a combustion engine is, or how a drive shaft performs, but we use automobiles, at least on most occasions, as a tool to benefit our daily lives.

It is not essential, we believe, that the businessman-manager understand exactly how computers work, for example. If he has a good general understanding of what they can do, he is not in bad shape. The same is true of the use of higher mathematics.

3. Sometime in the future, however, it is conceivable that the successful business manager will have to be completely conversant with higher mathematics, as one of the skills essential for success in the increasingly competitive marketplace. We suspect that this time is a long way off, in that so many business judgments, based upon available data, are much more qualitative than quantitative, and bright young men can be hired to find answers if the businessman knows enough to ask the right questions.

We believe that in the present state of the art, Operations Research has not been brought to the point where an entire enterprise can be modeled and answers to all its problems can come out of a computer. At the same time, we believe that the modeling of specific problems, some fairly broad in scope, can be helpful to businesses large and small.

Returning to the point of this book, planning and control of various segments of a business can be vastly improved by a systems analysis approach.

The preceding eight chapters have served as an introduction to the major mathematical concepts that together constitute the science of Operations Research. The approach we have taken has emphasized the assumptions, logic, and limitations of each of the techniques, and we have tried to make Operations Research a less forbidding topic.

If we have been at all successful in our efforts, we have convinced you that it is not the mathematics which should attract the primary interest of management, but instead it is the model which requires critical appraisal. It is the technician's job to handle the mathematics. In evaluating his work, however, it is the manager's job to assure himself that the model used is a satisfactory representation of the real-life situation; that is, to confirm that the assumptions are realistic, to question whether the simplifications made do not distort the picture, to decide whether the implied cause-and-effect relationships are true. It is also the manager's job to bring into consideration the qualitative factors which the study did not consider and which the problems of implementation might present.

A too-common misconception that we hope our approach has dispelled is the extreme position that some have taken; namely, that at some stage in its development Operations Research can be expected to do away with the traditional responsibilities of management. This simply is not the case. Operations Research merely consists of a number of analytic tools—to be sure, some very sophisticated tools—which supplement the tools management is presently using for planning and control.

The question is not whether you are or are not in favor of Operations Research, but whether you believe in the usefulness of systematic planning and control for the running of your business. Given that you are committed in this direction, the question becomes to what extent Operations Research can help. In this frame of mind you want to use it to whatever extent its limitations allow. In this respect, Operations Research might be viewed as being akin to the role of budgeting in the planning and control process. And we have never heard anyone claim that budgeting will someday replace management.

One final purpose we hope our approach has served is that of preparing you to make use of the extensive literature in the field. In concluding our discussion of Operations Research, then, we would like to invite you to make use of the reading list with which we close the chapter. Almost any good business library can make available to you the books and periodicals listed, and you should take advantage of them if you are interested in learning more about the technical aspects of Operations Research or about its applications.

Bibliography

P E R I O D I C A L S

Cors Journal, Canadian Operational Research Society, P.O. Box 2225, Station D, Ottawa, Ontario, Can.

Datamation, F. D. Thompson Publications, Inc., 141 E. 44 Street, New York, N.Y. 10017.

Harvard Business Review, Soldiers Field, Boston, Mass.

I.B.M. Systems Journal, Data Processing Division, 112 East Post Road, White Plains, N.Y. 10601.

Journal of Industrial Engineering, American Institute of Industrial Engineers, Inc., 345 E. 47 Street, New York 10017.

Management Science, The Institute of Management Sciences, P.O. Box 626, Ann Arbor, Mich.

Operations Research, Operations Research Society of America, Mount Royal and Guilford Avenues, Baltimore, Md. 21202.

Operations Research/Management Science, Executive Sciences Institute, Inc., Whippany, N.J.

A monthly digest service that abstracts articles and papers from both foreign and domestic periodicals and a number of symposiums. Coverage of the OR field is complete, précis *are good, indexed by technique and functional area. A regular reading of the digest provides an excellent way of keeping up with the development of the theory and practice, and of making sure you haven't missed any im-*

portant articles. Flip through the past four or five volumes to get a good feel for the state of the art. (If you are interested, a year's subscription is $75.)

BOOKS

Introductory

Management Science, A Primer for Managers, O. C. Nord and D. W. Parker, Management Science Associates, 1964.
A good summary approach to fundamentals of Operations Research with a number of examples which, though simple, get the important points across. Particularly interesting is the final chapter review of a questionnaire the authors mailed to the Fortune 500, in which meaningful comments about Operations Research from managers' points of view are made.

New Decision Making Tools for Managers, E. C. Bursk and J. F. Chapman, Harvard University Press, Cambridge, Mass., 1963.

Scientific Decision Making in Business, A. Schuchman, Holt Rinehart and Winston, New York, 1963.
Two highly readable books of articles. The articles are written primarily for the businessman, covering the spectrum of techniques and applications. A few articles have some mathematics, but none require prior knowledge in that everything is carefully explained.

Mathematics and Technical Background

Introduction to Operations Research, C. W. Churchman, R. L. Ackoff, and E. L. Arnoff, John Wiley & Sons, Inc., New York, 1957.
A classic textbook and reference work. Requires some mathematics background, but technical level is not prohibitive. Some excellent illustrations.

Introduction to Statistics for Business Situations, R. Schlaifer, McGraw-Hill Book Co., Inc., New York, 1961.
A good introduction to statistical analysis of decision problems. Requires some mathematical background.

Mathematics for Management Series, C. H. Springer, R. E. Herlihy, and R. I. Beggs, Richard D. Irwin, Inc., Homewood, Ill., 1965.
General Electric Company sponsored the four volumes in this series: Basic Mathematics, Advanced Methods and Models, Statistical Inference, Probabilistic Models. *Highly useful in developing "awareness and understanding of mathematical applications to business situations without requiring the individual to become a technician or practitioner." Will not make you a mathematician but will give you a solid background. Requires no initial mathematical ability. Highly readable.*

Operations Research—Methods & Problems, M. Sasieni, A. Yaspan, and L. Friedman, John Wiley & Sons, Inc., New York, 1959.
An alternative to Churchman's Introduction.

Production and Marketing

> *Mathematical Models and Marketing Management,* R. D. Buzzell, Harvard University Graduate School of Business Administration, Division of Research, Cambridge, Mass., 1964.
> *An absolute "must read" rating for managers. Focus is on a number of specific marketing applications, but the treatment yields a very good exposition of the role of Operations Research in management. If I had to recommend only one book, this would be the one.*

> *Models for Production and Operations Management,* E. S. Buffa, John Wiley & Sons, Inc., New York, 1963.
> *A not-too-technical coverage of the application of Operations Research in inventory, production, and distribution problems.*

Index

Accounting, ix–x, 3, 4, 27
  concepts of, changing, 42–44
    inventory valuations, 43
    loss of productivity of assets, 43
    passing the earnings statement, 43
    pension-plan liabilities, 43–44
    price levels, 42
    realization of income, timing of, 42–43
    regulated industries, accounting for, 43
    research and development costs, 44
  responsibility, 14–15, 73
  statements, *see* Statements, accounting
Accounting Corporation of America, 40
Accounts payable, 128
Accounts receivable, financing of, 127
Administrative costs, 98–105
  program budgeting, 99–100
  repetitive tasks, 100–4
    average actual, 101–2
    measurement programs, 100–1, 105
    motion analysis with predetermined times, 104
    random work sampling, 102–3
    time study, 103
Advertising expenditures, 34, 58–61
Alternative investments, ranking of, 107–9, 118–19

American Management Association, 92
Applied research, 91, 93–95
Arrival rate, queuing theory, 172
Assets, balance sheet, 28–29
  idle, disposition of, 129
  productivity of, loss of, 43
Assignment-of-orders problem, mathematical programming application, 201
Average-actual output, 101–2
Average annual return, 112, 113
Axe, the, development of, trial-and-error solution, 163–64

Balance sheet, 3, 27–32, 37, 38, 44, 45
  assets, 28–29
  book value, 29–30
  liabilities, 29
  limitations of, 28
  owner's equity, 29–32
  parts of, 28
  use of, 27–28
Bank collection services, cash availability, 126
Basic Motion Timestudy (BMT), data table, 104
Billing, cash availability, 126
Bill of materials, 68
Bonus awards, salesmen, 56–58
Book value, balance sheet, 29–30
Branch cash, controlling, 126
Break-even charts, 11–12

Bridge design, evolution of simulation, 164–66
Budget, 4–5, 13, 17–18
   cash, 123
   final, 65
   flexible, 10–11
   project, 105
   sales, final, preparation of, 51–52, 65
      preliminary, example of, 48–49
      preparation of, 47, 64
Budgetary control, x, 13–18
   management by exception, 15–17
   problem, typical, 16–17
   responsibility, accounting, 14–15
      factory overhead, 15
      sales expenses, 14–15
Budgeting, 65
   capital, 106–9
      alternative investments, ranking of, 107–9
      examples, practical, 116–18
      payback period, 109–12
      present-value concepts, 113–16
      rate of return, 112–13
   program, 99–100
Budget timetable, representative, 9–10
Burden, 73–75
Business Ratios (Dun & Bradstreet), 40

Capital budgeting, 106–19
   alternative investments, ranking of, 107–9
      considerations, general, 109
      dependent investments, 108
      independent investments, 108
      mutually exclusive investments, 107–8
   examples, practical, 116–18
      alternatives, choice of, 116–17
      existing conditions, comparison with, 117–18
   payback period, 109–12
      examples, 110–12
   present-value concepts, 113–16
   rate of return, 112–13
Capital investments, evaluation of, 129
Cash, 36–37
   availability of, improving, 123–27

   bank collection services, 126
   billing, 126
   branch cash, controlling, 126
   cash discount and credit, 126–27
   cash receipts, processing, 126
   vendor payments, 127
branch controlling, 126
flow of, 121–23
idle, use of, 129
management of, see Cash management
receipts and disbursements, projected, statement of, 124–25
Cash budget, 123
Cash discount, credit and, 126–27
Cash management, 120–30
   cash availability, improving, 123–27
      bank collection services, 126
      billing, 126
      branch cash, controlling, 126
      cash discount and credit, 126–27
      cash receipts, processing, 126
      vendor payments, 127
   cash budget, 123
   essentials of, 121
   financial management, 127–29
      accounts payable, 128
      accounts receivable, financing of, 127
      capital investments, evaluation of, 129
      customer financing, 127–28
      idle assets, disposition of, 129
      idle cash, use of, 129
      income tax policies, 129
      inventories, 128
      sale and leasebacks, 128
   flow of cash, 121–23
Cash receipts, processing, 126
Chance variation, queuing theory, 174–75
Charts, break-even, 11–12
Communication, 22, 23
Comparative ratios, data on, 40
Compensation plans, salesmen, 54–58
Conclusions, testing of, characteristic of Operations Research, 142

Constraints, factor of mathematical program, 200–1
Consumer demand, 9, 10, 46
Control, budgetary, x, 13–18
 management by exception, 15–17
 problem, typical, 16–17
 responsibility accounting, 14–15
 inventory, 69–70
 Operations Research in, usefulness of, 216–18
 pure and fundamental research, difficulties in, 92
Correlation, regression analysis and, 185
 business example, 186–88
 practical situation, 189–90
 uses of, 188–89
Cost centers, 73–74
Costing, incremental, 84–88
 example of, 86–88
Cost of goods sold, profit and loss statement, 32–34
Costs, administrative, 98–105
 program budgeting, 99–100
 repetitive tasks, 100–4
 cost-center, 74–75
 critical path scheduling, 212–15
 development, accounting for, 44
 distribution, 54–64
  advertising, 58–61
  direct selling, 54–58
  excess inventory, 63–64
  physical, 61–64
  promotion, 58–61
 overhead, 73–75
 research and development, 90
  accounting for, 44
 standard, 70–71, 75–84
  accountant's view of, 76
  case study of, 79–84
  manager's view of, 77
 See also Expenses
Credit, cash discount and, 126–27
Critical path, the, 210–12
Critical Path Measurement (CPM), 207, 208, 212
 advantages of using, 215
 control of program by, 215
Critical path scheduling, 205–15
 cost and other factors, 212–15
 critical path, the, 210–12

Critical Path Measurement (CPM), 207, 208, 212
 advantages of using, 215
 control of program by, 215
 one-of-a-kind projects, 207–9
 problem, practical, 209–10
 Project Evaluation and Review Technique (PERT), 207, 208, 209, 211, 212
 advantages of using, 215
 control of program by, 215
Current assets, 28–29
Current ratio, 38
Customer financing, 127–28
Customers, queuing theory, 172

Data tables, 104
Debt-to-equity ratio, 39
Decision variables, factor of mathematical program, 200
Defense Department, U.S., 207
Denisy, M., 165
Dependent investments, 108
Depreciation, 73
 profit and loss statement, 35
Development, 91, 96
 cost of, accounting for, 44
 expenses of, 90
 problem area of business, 21–22
Direct labor, costs of, 71–72
 standards, 72–73
Direct selling expenses, 54–58
Discount, cash, and credit, 126–27
 rate of, 114–15, 119
Distribution, costs of, 54–64
 advertising, 58–61
 direct selling, 54–58
 excess inventory, 63–64
 physical, 61–64
 promotion, 58–61
 types of, 50
Dun & Bradstreet, 40
Dynamic programming, 192

Earnings statement, see Profit and loss statement
Equity, net profit/stockholders', 40
 owner's or stockholders', balance sheet, 29–32
Excess inventory, cost of, 63–64
Expectancy, reasonable, concept of, 78

Expected values, 158–62
  probability measurements, sources
    of, 161–62
Expense accounts, salesmen, 58
Expenses, advertising, 58–61
  overhead, 73–75
  physical distribution, 61–64
  profit and loss statement, 34
  promotion, 58–61
  selling, direct, 54–58
  See also Costs

Factory overhead, responsibility ac-
    counting, 15
Federal Trade Commission, 40, 54
Feedback, 4
FIFO (first-in, first-out), 29, 33, 35,
    43
Finance, problem area of business,
    21
Financial management, 127–29
  accounts payable, 128
  accounts receivable, financing of,
    127
  capital investments, evaluation of,
    129
  customer financing, 127–28
  idle assets, disposition of, 129
  idle cash, use of, 129
  income tax policies, 129
  inventories, 128
  sale and leasebacks, 128
Financial statements, 14
Financing, accounts receivable, 127
  customer, 127–28
First-year return, 112, 113
Flexible budget, 10–11
Forecasts, 13
  product costs, 70
  sales, 47–48
Fundamental research, 91–93
  planning and controlling, difficul-
    ties in, 92
  values of, 93
Funds, source and application of,
    statement of, 36–38, 44

Gantt Charts, 205, 206
General expenses, 34
Graphs, 11–12
Gross National Product (GNP), 90

Idle assets, disposition of, 129
Idle cash, use of, 129
Incentive compensation plans, sales-
    men, 55–58
Income, realization of, timing of,
    42–43
Income statement, 32–34, 44, 45
  comparative, 34–36
  consumer products division, 17
  cost of goods sold, 32–34
  depreciation, 35
  elements of, 32
  expenses, 34
  inventories, 35
  over-all, 16
  over-all effects, 34–36
  taxes, 34, 35–36
  use of, 32–34
Income taxes, 34, 35–36
  policies, financial management, 129
Incremental costing, 84–88
  examples, 86–88
Independent investments, 108
Inference, *see* Statistical inference
Information, 19–23
Integer programming, 192
Interpretation of financial state-
    ments, 38–41
Inventories, 29, 33, 66
  evaluation of, 33–34
  excess, cost of, 63–64
  financial management, 128
  profit and loss statement, 35
Inventory control, 69–70
Inventory problem, Operations Re-
    search, 144–51
Inventory turnover, 39–40
Inventory valuation, 43
Investments, alternative, ranking of,
    118–19
  capital, evaluation of, 129
  dependent, 108
  independent, 108
  mutually exclusive, 107–8
Job shop, 67
Job standards, 55

Key Busineess Ratios (Dun & Brad-
    street), 40

Labor, direct, costs of, 71–72
  standards, 72–73

Leasebacks, sale and, financial management, 128
Liabilities, balance sheet, 29
pension-plan, 43–44
LIFO (last-in, first-out), 29, 33, 35, 36, 43
Linear programming, 192–93
Long-range plan, 4–5
Long-term control, 13
Loss, productivity of asset, 43

Management, cash, *see* Cash management
financial, *see* Financial management
Management by exception, 15–17
Management Information Systems, (MIS), 19–23
Marketing, 46–65
distribution, types of, 50
distribution costs, 54–64
advertising, 58–61
direct selling expenses, 54–58
excess inventory, 63–64
physical, 61–64
promotion, 58–61
price setting, 53–54
problem areas of business, 21, 49–51
sales budget, 47, 64
final, preparation of, 51–52, 65
preliminary, example of, 48–49
sales forecast, 47–48
sales revenues, 47–54
Materials, 68–71
bill of, 68
buying, 68–69
inventory control, 69–70
pricing, 70–71
standard-cost system for, 70–71
Mathematical analysis, 193
Mathematical programming, 192–204
application of, 201–2
complications of, 202–4
features of, basic, 200–1
limitations of, 202–4
logic of, 199–200
meaning of, 194
shipping problem, 194–98
Measurement, characteristic of Operations Research, 141–42

probability, sources of, 161–62
Measurement programs, 100–1, 105
Methods-Time Measurement (MTM), data table, 104
Models, use of, characteristic of Operations Research, 142
Morris Associates, Robert, 40
Motion analysis with predetermined times, 104
Mutually exclusive investments, 107–8

Net profit/stockholders' equity, 40
Net-sales-to-inventory ratio, 39–40
Net worth, balance sheet, 29–30
New York Stock Exchange, 29
Notes on financial statements, 35–36, 44

Objective function, factor of mathematical program, 200
Objectivity, characteristic of Operations Research, 141
Obsolescence, 69
One-of-a-kind projects, critical path scheduling, 207–9
Operations Research (OR), ix, x, 3, 4, 22, 23, 133
characteristics of, 141–42
conclusions, testing of, 142
measurement, 141–42
models, use of, 142
objectivity, 141
critical path scheduling, 205–15
cost and other factors, 212–15
critical path, the, 210–12
Critical Path Measurement (CPM), 207, 208, 212, 215
one-of-a-kind projects, 207–9
problem, practical, 209–10
Project Evaluation and Review Technique (PERT), 207, 208, 209, 211, 212, 215
inventory problem, 144–51
mathematical programming, 192–204
applications of, 200–1
complications of, 202–4
features of, basic, 200–1
limitations of, 202–4
logic of, 199–200
meaning of, 194
shipping problem, 194–98

Operations Research (*cont'd.*)
  meaning of, 133–39
  queuing theory, 171–80
    chance variation, 174–75
    decision, the, 173
    model, the, 172–73
    problem, the, 173–74
    solution, method of, 175–80
  risk factor, handling, 152–62
    expected values, 158–62
    least regret, criterion of, 155–56
    optimism, criterion of, 154–55
    pessimism, criterion of, 154
    probability as a yardstick, 156–58
    probability measurements, sources of, 161–62
  shipping problem, 135–39
  solutions established by, 139–40
  statistical inference, 181–91
    probability, sampling and, 182–85
    regression analysis, correlation and, 185–90
    sampling, 181–82
  system simulation, 163–70, 175
    business problem, 167–70
    evolution of, 164–66
    principles of, 166–67
    trial-and-error solution, 163–64
    waiting-line problem, 176–80
  tool of planning, 133–43
  usefulness of, in planning and control, 216–18
  use of, 140–41
Order-takers, 55
Other assets, 28, 29
Over-all income statement, 16
Overhead, costs of, 73–75
Owner's equity, balance sheet, 29–32

Payback period, examples, capital budgeting, 109–12
Pension-plan liabilities, 43–44
Personnel, administrative, 98–99
Physical distribution expenses, 61–64
Planning, 6–12
  accounting as handmaiden of, 7
  break-even charts, 11–12
  budget timetable, representative, 9–10

flexible budget, 10–11
long-range, 4–5
objectives, setting, 8
Operations Research as tool of, 133–43
  usefulness of, 216–18
problem, typical, 8–9
pure and fundamental research, difficulties in, 92
qualitative and quantitative, 6–8
time to be spent in, 6
Polaris missile, 207
Present-value concepts, capital budgeting, 113–16
Price levels, changing, 42
Probability, means of quantifying risk, 156–58
  measurements, sources of, 161–62
  sampling and, 182–85
Process industries, 66–67
Product-mix problem, mathematical programming application, 201
Production, 66–89
  elements of, 67–75
    direct labor, 71–73
    materials, 68–71
    overhead, 73–75
  incremental costing, 84–88
    examples, 86–88
  limitations to, 67
  problem area of business, 21
  standard costs, 75–84
    accountant's view of, 76
    case study of, 79–84
    manager's view of, 77
Productive capacity, 9
Productivity of assets, loss of, 43
Profit, 46
Profit and loss statement, 3, 27, 32–34, 37, 44, 45
  comparative, 34–36
  cost of goods sold, 32–34
  depreciation, 35
  elements of, 32
  expenses, 34
  inventories, 35
  over-all effects, 34–36
  passing the, 43
  revenues, 32
  taxes, 34, 35–36
  use of, 32–34

Profit-sharing, compensation plan for salesmen, 58
Program budgeting, 99–100
Programming, mathematical, *see* Mathematical programming
Project budget, 105
Project Evaluation and Review Technique (PERT), 207, 208, 209, 211, 212
advantages of using, 215
control of program by, 215
Promotion expenditures, 58–61
Pure research, 90, 91–93
planning and controlling, difficulties in, 92
values of, 93

Quadratic programming, 192
Queue discipline, 172
Queuing theory, 171–80
chance variation, 174–75
decision, the, 173
model, the, 172–73
problem, the, 173–74
waiting-line, simulation solution to, 176–80
solution, method of, 175–76
simulation, 176–80
Quick ratio, 38

Random work sampling, 102–3
Ranking of alternative investments, 107–9, 118–19
Rate of discount, 114–15, 119
of return, capital budgeting, 112–13
Ratio analysis, 38–41
comparative ratios, data on, 40
current ratio, 38
debt-to-equity ratio, 39
net profit/stockholders' equity, 40
net-sales-to-inventory ratio, 39–40
quick ratio, 38
Realization of income, timing of, 42–43
Reasonable expectancy, concept of, 78
Regression analysis, correlation and, 185
business example, 186–88
practical situation, 189–90
uses of, 188–89

Regulated industries, accounting for, 43
Repetitive tasks, administrative costs of, 100–4
average actual, 101–2
measurement programs, 100–1, 105
motion analysis with predetermined times, 104
random work sampling, 102–3
time study, 103
Research, 90–96
applied, 91, 93–95
cost of, accounting for, 44
expenses of, 90
fundamental, 91–93
planning and controlling, difficulties in, 92
values of, 93
measurement of, 95
Operations Research, *see* Operations Research
problem area of business, 21–22
pure, 90, 91–93
planning and controlling, difficulties in, 92
values of, 93
quantitative analysis of, 95
Responsibility accounting, 14–15, 73
Return, rate of, capital budgeting, 112–13
Revenues, profit and loss statement, 32
sales, *see* Sales revenues
Risk factor, handling, Operations Research
expected values, 158–62
least regret, criterion of, 155–56
optimism, criterion of, 154–55
pessimism, criterion of, 154
probability as a yardstick, 156–58
probability measurements, sources of, 161–62
Rule of thumb, 38, 39, 70

Sale and leasebacks, financial management, 128
Sales budget, final, preparation of, 51–52, 65
preliminary, example of, 48–49
preparation of, 47, 64

Sales expenses, responsibility accounting, 14–15
Sales forecast, 47–48
Salesmen, compensation plans, 54–58
  expense accounts, 58
Sales revenues, 47–54
  price setting, 53–54
  problem areas, possible, 49–51
  sales budget, 47, 64
    final, preparation of, 51–52, 65
    preliminary, example of, 48–49
  sales forecast, 47–48
Sampling, 181–82
  probability and, 182–85
  random work, 102–3
  reasons for using, 182
Scheduling, see Critical path scheduling
Securities and Exchange Commission, 40, 85
Selling expenses, direct, 34, 54–58
Service capacity, queuing theory, 172
Shipping problem, Operations Research, 135–39
Short-term control, 13
Simulation, see Systems simulation
Source and application of funds, statement of, 36–38, 44
Standard costs, 70–71, 75–84
  accountant's view of, 76
  case study of, 79–84
  manager's view of, 77
Standard hours, 72
Standards, direct labor, 72–73
  job, 55
Statements, accounting, balance sheet, see Balance sheet
  limitations of, 40
  profit and loss, see Profit and loss statement
  source and application of funds, 36–38, 44
  cash receipts and disbursements, projected, 124–25
  financial, 14
    interpretation of, 38–41
    notes on, 35–36, 44
  income, see Income statement
  profit and loss, see Profit and loss statement

Statement Studies (Robert Morris Associates), 40
Statistical inference, 181–91
  regression analysis, correlation and, 185
    business example, 186–88
    practical situation, 189–90
    uses of, 188–89
  sampling, 181–82
    probability and, 182–85
Stillman, Charles L., 14
Stochastic programming, 192
Stockholders' equity, balance sheet, 29–32
System simulation, 163–70, 175
  business problem, 167–70
  evolution of, 164–66
  principles of, 166–67
  trial-and-error solution, 163–64
  waiting-line problem, 176–80
    solution to, 175–80

Taxes, income, 34, 35–36
  policies, financial management, 129
  profit and loss statement, 34, 35–36
Time study, 103
Total return, 112, 113
Trial-and-error solution, system simulation, 163–64
"Trim waste"-in-a-paper-mill problem, mathematical programming application, 201–02

Valuations, inventory, 43
Value, book, balance sheet, 29–30
  expected, probability measurements, sources of, 161–62
  present, concepts of, capital budgeting, 113–16
Variation, chance, queuing theory, 174–75
Vendor payments, cash availability, 127

Waiting-line problem, 171–72, 173–75
  simulation solution to, 175–80
Walker, S. Branch, 113
Work Factor (WF) data table, 104
World War II, x, 3